HARRY DOLMAN

THE MILLIONAIRE INVENTOR WHO BECAME "MR BRISTOL CITY"

Martin Powell & Clive Burlton

Bristol Books CIC
The Courtyard, Wraxall Hill, Wraxall, Bristol, BS48 1NA

Harry Dolman
written and researched by Martin Powell
additional writing and research by Clive Burlton

Published by Bristol Books 2017

ISBN: 9781909446144

Design: Joe Burt

Printed by Hobbs the Printers Ltd, Totton, Hampshire

CONTENTS

Foreword by Marina Dolman MBE   7

Country Boy   9
Wiltshire Yeoman   19
Apprentice to Director   36
The Flying Flea   52
War, Peace and Football   59
Ashton Gate   74
Managers, Men and Management   83
Atyeo and Promotion   94
The Man with the Midas Touch   103
Marina   116
The Sixties   127
The Dolman Stand   142
Stepping Down   167
Mr Bristol City   179
Standing Ovation   189

Acknowledgements   197
Picture Credits   199

FOREWORD
BY MARINA DOLMAN MBE

Harry Dolman was a remarkable man, who meant different things to so many different people. We enjoyed wonderful years as husband and wife and it was always fascinating to hear him talk about the days before I knew him, building up his business and his passion for Bristol City Football Club.

I always thought it would make a lovely book and now, 40 years after his death, here it is! The final decision came from a casual conversation with Clive Burlton while looking at the aeroplane Harry built – The Flying Flea – which hangs in M Shed museum, Bristol.

During research for the book, I was thrilled to re-discover Harry's hand-written notes with his version of events. Some were drafts for speeches he gave, others just recollections he jotted down for his own amusement and record. They make this account of his life more accurate than we could ever have imagined.

Many images reproduced in the book were found in the little overnight case that Harry used to take to Bristol City away games. Other finds have included a marvellous photograph album that Harry was compiling about Brecknell, Dolman and Rogers, and a vinyl recording about Bristol City's 1954-55 promotion season.

My thanks to Martin Powell and Clive Burlton for taking all this information, along with their own research, and writing and compiling a book that does justice to Harry's fascinating life.

Harry was blessed with a great deal of common sense – the most I've ever come across in a man. He could think through situations and find a solution in a way that was remarkable and rare, which is why he came up with so many innovations and inventions.

He was also forward-looking and constantly predicting the future and was so often right about how the world – and particularly the business and football world - would develop.

I miss him very much and hope that this book in some way helps to preserve his memory and show others how much one man with determination and talent can achieve.

COUNTRY BOY

I t was on August 6, 1897, that Charlie Dolman, landlord of The Brewery Tap in the Wiltshire village of Langley Burrell, heard the first cry of his latest child. His wife Ann had gone into labour and soon a gaggle of local women announced to him that it was a boy.

He already had a six-year-old son, who carried his own name, Charles, and two daughters; Laura, aged three, and Kate, aged two. He and Ann settled on the names Henry James for this latest bundle of joy.

Charlie was 32 and was a Wiltshire man by birth, having been born in the village of Charlton. He had moved north to Chesterfield to work as an insurance agent with the Wesleyan General Insurance company but after six years returned to his native Wiltshire to become a publican and work the land.

No doubt some glasses were raised at The Brewery Tap, now The Langley Tap, that night in the quiet little village just a couple of miles from Chippenham.

Charlie was a country man at heart and loved nothing better than getting the most out of the land. Not long after baby Henry was born he moved the family to take over the Plume of Feathers, now The Old Plume, in the village of Burton. Soon after that he moved again to Yatton Keynell where he took over as landlord of The Bell Inn and where he could also farm on a small piece of land, keeping dairy cattle and growing crops.

Charles Dolman knew the village well. He had been brought up there and his first job was farm work for Mr John Marsh of Manor Farm. He was to stay at The Bell Inn for the next 30 years while also farming at nearby Sparrow's Farm.

Originally an old farmhouse, The Bell was capable of housing his ever growing family. The 1911 census shows the Dolman family had grown by three more children by that time, all living at home: Charles Junior, now 19; Laura, now 16; Kate, aged 15; Henry, 13; John, always known as Jack, 11; Victor, aged 10, and Arthur, aged four. Little Arthur had an accident when he was very young and as a result was blind. He was the youngest of the seven children.

The Bell Inn had a history dating back to the 17th Century and originally had a brewhouse. It had a garden and an orchard and, 30 years before Charlie Dolman took over, a previous landlord had been both a publican and the local butcher.

The Dolman family was a well-known and well-liked major part of the Yatton Keynell village scene.

From an early age Henry was affectionately known as Harry and he learned a lot from his father that was to stay with him for the rest of his days. At the age of 10 Harry would be helping his father milk the cows before taking himself off to school, gaining a work ethic from his father. He was also learning the value of money and how to negotiate.

Harry once went out with his father on a shopping trip where his father bought nine pairs of shoes, a pair for each of the children, and a pair each for himself and his wife Ann.

Harry told the story years later:

"I don't remember the exact price but it was something like one pound and fourpence-halfpenny for the nine pairs. The shopkeeper wrapped them up and waited for the money.

"My father said: 'You'll take off the fourpence halfpenny of course'. The shopkeeper protested but my father pointed out he didn't often sell nine pairs at once and, of course, my father won. I was embarrassed, I didn't know where to put myself. I was only a lad of about ten."

But it was a lesson Harry learned from and was to put into practice many times over the years. Although he adopted his father's enthusiasm for business and doing deals it was obvious from a very young age that he didn't share his father's enthusiasm for the land. Harry Dolman preferred machines. He liked the way they worked. He liked the way they made life easier for just about every task; how a series of cogs, switches and pulleys could help with a rural task. He had an inventive mind and many ideas for machines that could revolutionise the way people lived - making life easier and saving some of the back-breaking work of country life.

He wrote this account of his early days:

"Nothing very eventful happened in my young school days. I remember two things. I was particularly fond of football and I was terribly fascinated with engines. Many a time I got a hiding for being very late home due to the fact I just couldn't drag myself away from the football field. My mother thought it was a game for hooligans and roughnecks and my father thought it was more important that I should spend all my spare time doing something useful. Consequently I did more than my share of work, for a young schoolboy.

"However any spare time I did get was spent playing football or messing about with machinery of some kind. The chaff cutter and the mowing machine were all taken to pieces at some time or other. One occasion I was almost scared stiff when I found that I could not fit some part or other back together properly and as I had dismantled the machines without my father's knowledge I used to beg my elder brother Charley to come and put the job right.

"My strong points at school were arithmetic, painting and drawing but I was very backward in all other subjects. The older I became the more I loved school and, on reaching the age of 14 when I was due to leave, I asked my father to let me continue at school afternoons only and I helped him with the work at home mornings. This continued until I was 14 and a quarter.

"I hated the work at home feeding and attending the pigs, fouls, milking cows and the hundred and one other jobs in a small holding which my father ran as well as keeping a local pub. My younger brother Jack was more fitted for the work at home. My father would go roundabout on 18 other farms to buy a number of pigs and Jack and I would have to fetch them. It was usual to ask the sellers of the pigs for one shilling. My father said this was known as "lunch money". Jack my brother always asked for it but I wasn't so brave so often did not get it. On more than one occasion I got a cut with a whip and cane for not asking for this wretched shilling "lunch money". I remember on one occasion I hadn't asked for it and, when I arrived home with the pigs, father said: "Did you ask for the lunch money" and to dodge a hiding I said "yes". "Did he give it to you?" continued my father. I again lied and said "yes" then he said "where is it?" Needless to say I continued to lie and was given a hiding and sent to bed without my tea. "You'll never get on" said my father.

"The more I saw of pigs and fouls the more I hated the work at home with the exception of the pony. I spent hours grooming, feeding and looking after the pony. The pony grew fond of me because he would come to me in the field where he grazed whereas no-one else could get within yards of him."

Luckily in the village there was an established steam roller manufacturer and agricultural engineering business called Hulands, Robert and Sons. In the Wiltshire trade directory of 1875 Robert Huland was classed as a "blacksmith, engineer and agricultural machinist". He had an engineer, engine driver and machinist working for him. By 1909 it was a small and thriving engineering business serving the local farms, with young Harry doing little jobs and studying intently the engineering work he saw going on around him.

Harry, with his insatiable appetite for machinery and engineering, was soaking up all he could from being part of the village business that served the agricultural community in the area.

He described those days:

"It was my dislike for the work at home that started my life as an engineer and at 14 and a half years of age I started as an apprentice at the local agricultural engineering works. I was paid a shilling per week starting work at seven in the morning and finishing at five, seven to one on Saturdays. It was a very small works employing about 15 people. The machinery was crude but they did a little of everything and I think I learned more in the 18 months there than in any other 18 months of my life. I was taught moulding, turning, milling, drilling, forging and a little carpentry work. I helped with the sawing of tree trunks, in fact my job was looking after the steam engines which drove the circular saw. I was really in my element but there was one snag - one shilling a week, which was increased to two after one year.

"A friend of mine with whom I used to play football was working at the same works. He was not apprenticed and was being paid 10 shillings a week. I just could not understand why there was such a difference and although I was supposed to be tied for five years my indentures had not been signed due to an oversight of the boss so I begged my father to let me leave. My boss was very upset and did his best to make me stay but I had made up my mind."

Besides engineering Harry continued his passion for football. Every Saturday he would hurry home from work at lunchtime, change into his football togs in his room in the Bell Inn, then walk several miles to play for Yatton Keynell at the sport he loved. He was a centre-forward and loved nothing better than the thrill of scoring goals. Those early games for the village team started a playing career that spanned decades.

All through his working life he found time for football. He finally hung up his boots as a player when he was 40. As a 12-year-old with a passion for football living in the West Country he couldn't fail to hear about the exploits of the professional club in the big city to the west. Bristol City reached the FA Cup Final in 1909. Excitement reached fever pitch and West Country fans, some of them from Chippenham and the villages around, made their way to the Crystal Palace ground where a crowd of 71,000 watched Bristol City do battle with a team from Lancashire that were also making their first ever appearance in the cup - Manchester United.

The cup had captured the imagination of football fans over the last 38 years and the final was now established as the big game of the year. This year there would be a new name on the cup and those in the South West anticipated it would be the name of Bristol City, rather than the club from the North.

Both Bristol City and Manchester United usually played in red, so it was decided they should both change their strip for the big game - Bristol City opting for blue shirts while Manchester United played in white with a red V on the front.

Young Harry would have been influenced by hearing tales of the exploits of Billy Wedlock, nicknamed Fatty, the star of the Bristol City team, who was England's centre-half and would surely stop the Manchester United side winning.

But it was not to be Wedlock's day. Midway through the first half Sandy Turnbull, the Manchester United inside left, scored the only goal of the game after latching on to a rebound off the cross-bar to put the ball past City goalkeeper Harry Clay. Manchester United lifted the famous trophy for the first time in their history and the City fans returned to the West Country - maybe even to The Bell Inn, where Harry eagerly awaited tales of the game - to talk about what might have been and to predict that City would be back stronger than ever next year, and soon it would be their turn to win the cup.

Maybe a young lad today might decide that such a stunning victory would persuade him to support Manchester United for the rest of his days. But from all the evidence the big game sparked feelings in Harry for Bristol City. He could not possibly know at that stage of his life how intertwined his story would be with the trials and tribulations of that football club as they strived to reach the top.

For now his football dream revolved around scoring for Yatton Keynell: who knows, maybe one day being discovered to play for Bristol City. But deep down, like all teenage boys, he knew the most important thing was to learn his trade and get a job - after all there was never likely to be much money to be made from kicking a ball around for Bristol City or Manchester United!

He became an apprentice with Saxby & Farmer. The company was a major force in engineering and soon became part of Westinghouse Brake Company - and young Harry Dolman enjoyed working in the machine shop on railway projects, learning his trade. He said of the move to Saxby & Farmer:

"The intention was to apprentice me, providing I was satisfactory, after a probationary period. But no one worried and the probationary period lasted until I was mobilised in 1914. During the time I was with the Westinghouse Brake Company I was very happy. I improved my engineering knowledge considerably and my keenness resulted in my going to evening classes at the Chippenham Technical School.

"Some days I attended many classes, which meant I left home in the morning at 6.40am and would arrive home in the evening about

10 pm but I was now getting 11 shillings a week plus a four shilling bonus. My mother took 10 shillings the rest was pocket money for me so it paid me to work hard to earn a little bonus.

"My father and mother were good parents although they made me work hard, discipline was strict and I attended church or Sunday School every Sunday. The family was well looked after in every way and with my Grandma and a maid being with us there were 11 sitting down to every meal. We always had a side of bacon hanging in the kitchen and a large kitchen garden which kept the family in plenty of veg.

"My mother in fact was the kindest and most giving lady I have ever known - she would do without herself to help others and she worked very hard indeed all her life. She died from cancer at the age of 64. My father was a hard task master but he also had a very kind streak and did everything he was able to do to help all members of the family and I only heard him swear once in my life. He was forever telling me there was only one way to get on in life and that was to work hard. He died at 94 years of age. He started driving a car after the age of 60 and drove for 25 years. Although he spanked me many times when I'm sure I hardly deserved it, I remember both of my parents as two of the greatest people I have ever known."

As Harry Dolman worked through his teenage years Britain was spending money on building up its military strength and military uniforms were a common sight. Harry was too young to join up so he did the next best thing, as he explained:

"I always was fond of soldiers and sailors from early childhood. I think it must have been the uniform because when the opportunity came to join the Boy Scouts in 1912 two of my brothers and I applied to become members of a Boy Scout brigade at Castle Combe, two miles away from my home that meant that we had to walk that distance to do any training.

"To pay for our uniform we used to go out stone picking at one shilling a day on an estate in the village of Castle Combe - all three of us just managed to buy the Boy Scouts hat - that was as far as it got!"

Harry was now growing into a man and there was another interest that was to stay with him for the rest of his life, alongside football and machinery. The family's live-in maid had her attractions. In his personal memoirs written years later he confessed to his first encounter with the opposite sex and how his negotiation and mechanical skills played a part. It was while he was working at Westinghouse. Harry wrote:

"I should have allowed myself about half an hour to get to work but almost invariably left myself about 20 minutes to cycle the four miles. This meant that I was frequently a bit late which wasn't to my credit. However I got away with it and was never locked out as was the custom in those days. When I came home in the evening it was usual for us to have a hot meal, which my mother had put by for us at midday.

"The meal was put into the oven about half hour before my arrival and was served up by the maid we employed at that time. This girl was about 18, short and plump with a ripe fresh country looking complexion and at the same time a pleasant personality. It was not unusual for us to flirt together.

"One thing I remember clearly was that she would bring the tea pot over to me to pour my second cup. When passing the tea she would press her bosom into my face as I was sitting in the chair. I also very well remember she had large breasts and big nipples which seemed to dig into my cheek and on one occasion I grabbed her blouse pulled it down and nipped her nipple with my teeth. This sort of saucy play started something between us and at 16 I was trying hard to have relations with her and although she kept teasing me she firmly refused.

"Then one day she wanted to borrow my sister's bike and I persuaded my sister to lend the bike to her. The next morning she was worried because she'd had the misfortune to let the bike fall and damage the pedal crank. The result was that the pedal would not go round. She told me of this and asked if I would put the bike right without my sister knowing. I knew I could easily rectify the fault because the same thing had happened to my own bike and my brother had shown me how to put it right. So I started to bargain with her.

"My mother and father were both out and I was alone in the house with her and she gave me a promise that if I put the bike right I could have intercourse with her. I soon put the bike right and spent 10 minutes with her laying on some dirty washing. It was my first experience and how wonderful that was.

"My mother and father returned earlier than expected and I was lucky not to be caught but I was worried for the next three weeks. I was sure I was going to become a father. However everything was all right and I never repeated the act - not so much that I did not want to but mainly because the opportunity did not arise and soon after I joined up for the First World War."

WILTSHIRE YEOMAN

The Royal Wiltshire Yeomanry had a proud history of service as a cavalry unit. It had its headquarters at The Butts in London Road, Chippenham. In 1908 it became part of the Territorial Force and in 1913 was recruiting for young part-time soldiers.

On November 12, 1913, Harry and a group of others from work joined up. They became junior cavalry soldiers with drills locally. He told the story:

"My father allowed me to take a horse belonging to him which undoubtedly was perfect for the job. I had been riding it on and off for some time. We used to have mounted drill on Saturday afternoon and the first time I rode off from home on this horse was not exactly in keeping with a soldier of the King. I had to pass a field belonging to my father where I frequently took this nag in the evenings where it was left until required again.

"On this particular Saturday afternoon when I reached the gate of the field the horse wanted to be turned out into the field as usual and could I get it to pass that gate? I was afraid to use the spurs I was wearing in case it started to get frisky. In the end I turned back and asked my eldest brother to help. He mounted the horse and I rode a bike.

"Just before he arrived at the gate he used a stick on the horse which went galloping past. We then changed mounts and he returned on the bike and I proceeded to Chippenham for my first training. I enjoyed it very much but felt a little afraid because I didn't think the horse enjoyed it. When the training was over I had to ride the four miles back home but I had no further trouble. Sometimes it was not convenient to my father to take his horse and I had to ride a horse hired for the job. I was always apprehensive until I got used to the procedure."

In the months in the lead-up to war Harry went on a camp to Tisbury on Salisbury Plain. It was the first time he had been away from home and at just 16 he and a few other young lads found it tough as older soldiers arranged fights between them and introduced them to drink. Harry had sampled beer at haymaking time at home but found he couldn't keep up with his new drinking companions. He painted a fascinating picture of life in the camp:

"I remember that my closest friend was a young farmer who couldn't read and write. He used to ask me to read the letters he received from his girl. I also wrote his love letters for him. I felt most embarrassed because he would want some of the letters she had sent to him read time and again and when I was writing letters for him it would take hours and to make matters worse I was a bad speller and not a good writer but I did my best for him and the surprising thing was that his girlfriend did not know of his incapabilities.

"The young farmer was also a teetotaller which did not please some of the other men. They were determined to get him drunk. About the fourth day at camp one evening they pinned him to the ground with his legs and arms and poured beer into his mouth, much of which he had to swallow. I stood and watched and felt terrible but I'm glad to say that he stood his ground thereafter and stuck to his teetotal principles.

"When the war started he left the Yeomanry because it was considered farming was more important in those days; education was not very important and a farm man had to educate himself. This camp life was an eye opener for me. I was taught to drink, gamble and scrounge, the latter was deemed necessary for every soldier. I was bad at all three. I was a poor card player because I was too trusting and inexperienced and invariably lost. I was a poor drinker because I was too young and I was a poor scrounger because I had no courage for this method of obtaining things - but I was learning fast."

Yeomanry squadrons comprised 227 men and as a part-time soldier Harry attended parades, did weekly evening drills and went on occasional weekend camps while still working full time at Saxby & Farmer conscientiously completing his apprenticeship.

When, on August 4, 1914, Great Britain declared war on Germany and the First World War began Harry was among the first to step up from being a part-time soldier to a full-time soldier. His military record shows that he was "embodied" on August 5, 1914 - the day before his 17th birthday - which meant he became a full-time soldier right at the outset of the war.

Part-time soldiers were not compelled to sign up at that stage, but Harry did. He was keen to serve alongside many other men who volunteered for the 57 Yeomanry regiments, their manpower largely drawn from the rural and farming communities of their respective counties.

Fourteen young men from the little village of Yatton Keynell, or with parents who lived in the village, died during the war, a massive toll on a small rural community. Without a doubt Harry would have known some of those men, maybe went to school with them, or chatted to them as they drank in his father's pub.

But that was never the aspect of the First World War that he dwelled on when he talked about it in later years. For him it was a time of hard work, interest, comradeship and excitement. He threw himself into army life with enthusiasm. He told of how he went to war:

"On Monday, August 5, 1914, I went to work as usual. There were rumours of war breaking out with Germany but I had not taken much notice of the rumours and remarks by people of the possibility of war.

"But as soon as I started to operate the lathe I was working on friends around me asked me why I hadn't joined up. Evidently others had received their call up papers. I was told that the war had started and that it was certain my papers were awaiting me at home. I had left home at 6.40am before the post was delivered and as the morning wore away I began to wonder what to do. Some of my mates said "shove off home, you are bound to be mobilised" others said: "wait until this evening". By now I had that feeling of adventure so off I went clocking off without asking the foreman.

"When I arrived home half an hour later sure enough my calling up papers were there. It was my mother's birthday and she objected to my going. I was not 17 until the next day. I had now made my mind up and before I could get into uniform someone had called and instructed my father that our horse would be required and we had no option but to let it go.

"My parents had just bought me a new suit, the first made to measure I had ever possessed. My father's last words to me were: "I shall give your suit to Vic", my younger brother. "You won't be back for five years".

"I put on my uniform packed a few things in an old case and reported at the Chippenham Drill Hall. I left to go to war on the horse which I had been riding at the territorial camp only three months earlier. I was so proud of this horse, it was so much better than most but within a week it was taken from me.

"The major of our squadron was inspecting us from the centre of a large circle of us riding around in single file. He pointed to me to come near to him and commanded me to dismount. He said he thought the horse was too big for me - or I was too small for the horse - and a few days after I had to hand it over to his batman. The horse was now the major's mount. The one I got eventually was a rather little Argentine pony. I could have cried but there it was. I worried about this for days. I was in the army now and had to do what I was told.

"The first week we stayed in hotels and pubs at Chippenham, were partly equipped, then went to Winchester and were stationed at the college. One blanket between four. No milk in the tea. Very poor rations and what we did get I couldn't eat. We slept on the hard wood block floor of the gymnasium. Needless to say we slept with most of our clothes on. We had been given £5 mobilisation fee and most of us had taken our life savings with us so that we weren't short of money; consequently we did not go short of food.

"We were allowed to use the college swimming pool and altogether it was an enjoyable time. Furthermore everyone was so kind and generous. I remember more than one person saying: "you shouldn't be allowed in the army". I was 17 and looked younger.

"We stayed only a few days at Winchester and then moved on to Southampton where we were billeted in private houses. But it wasn't very long before we were under canvas, about 14 occupying each tent. We were allowed one blanket to two men; the food was a little better but the weather and sleeping conditions were atrocious. We remained under these conditions until about the end of November. We then went into new huts at Forest Row in Sussex. This was heavenly after the rough times we had experienced. By now I had become a hardened Yeoman drawing one shilling a day, all found.

"As already mentioned I had joined the gamblers, but I almost invariably lost mainly because of my inexperience, but partly because of the dishonesty of some of my comrades.

"One old soldier said to me: "If you must gamble buy a Crown and Anchor board and you will never be short of money." Up until that time I was always writing to my mother for subs as I was owing money to many of my friends. So I took the old soldier's tip and bought the Crown and Anchor board.

"Crown and Anchor of course was against many regulations and I was liable to heavy punishment. But I took the chance and was never short of money again during the remainder of my time in England. In fact I had so much money I felt ashamed of the fact that I had won it from my friends, although some of them had robbed me of pounds.

"I sailed for France towards the end of 1915 and vowed I would never gamble again whilst in the army and the Crown and Anchor board was thrown overboard."

The records show that on December 3, 1915, Harry joined the British Expeditionary Force. Two days later he landed at Le Havre in France and a short while later he entered the trenches.

Harry's service in the First World War earned him three medals: the 1914-15 Star, awarded to those who served in any theatre of war between August 5, 1914, and December 32, 1915; the British War Medal 1914-1918; and the Victory Medal. This medal set was affectionately and irreverently known as "Pip, Squeak and Wilfred". When medals were handed out in 1920 there was a popular Daily Mirror cartoon of that name, featuring Pip the dog, Squeak the penguin and Wilfred, a young rabbit. With many thousands of servicemen earning this particular set the nickname stuck and was a way of under-playing the importance of the awards.

Within a week of arriving in France Harry was at the trenches, often behind the front line looking after the horses. He was still boyish looking but even though he was among the youngest he was longing to get a commission and become a leader of men. He told of conditions in the early months of 1916, how he became one of the 20,000 British soldiers that succumbed to trench foot, and his first experience of the war:

"We had been in and out of the trenches for some weeks and I was beginning to learn something about war. I think I preferred going up to the front line rather than staying behind looking after 10 or 12 horses. It was much more exciting and as we had had a quiet time there seemed little danger providing you didn't do anything stupid. The worst part was the very cold, and in some places flooded, trenches.

"If you were unlucky enough to get stuck in a flooded trench it was usual to be issued with a pair of dry waders which reached your thighs. It was usual to collect these on the way up to the line. We were marched to a great heap of these waders then it was up to everyone to find himself a pair which were a reasonable fit as well as being waterproof.

"Many of them were leaky, which was not always apparent; many men came away with two left foots or two right-footed waders and just wore them happily, providing they were large enough and did not leak. On one occasion I was unlucky enough to have one leaky wader and after spending three days and two nights with a wet leg and foot I was terribly glad to go back out of it, and then I developed a bad attack of flu and trench foot.

"I was taken back behind the lines to a casualty clearing station which was a large marquee filled to the brim with camp beds. One was allocated to me and I was told to undress. My clothes were sent off to be fumigated and I was marched off to a place outside the marquee to have a wash from head to toe.

"I was really feeling terrible, the water was only just off the chill and it was very cold. When I got back to my cot I was so glad to get into the blankets but I couldn't get warm, in fact I was shivering with the cold. A blanket was taken from the next bed which surprised me until I realised another of my comrades had passed on.

"The food was plentiful and reasonably good and within a few days I was getting better. Then at lunchtime I got the shock of my life.

I was asked by the orderly if I would like a bottle of Guinness. I just could not believe it. He assured me I could have one and I don't think I have ever enjoyed a drink so much.

"As soon as I became well enough I had to help with the chores and then I was longing to get out of the place and back to my regiment. In fact I now hated the place. Soldiers were being carried out for the last time by the dozens - they weren't all as lucky as I was - and I had to help carry them out.

"I only went into the trenches once more after my short illness. The regiment was employed as traffic control, ammunition guards, carriers for ammo and other supplies to the front line and despatch riding, a job I got landed with, far away from the main squadron. Two of us were dumped near some very large guns. I think they were naval guns intended for long distance firing. What a terrific noise they made. How our horses stood it I shall never know. The Germans had similar guns firing back. The shell on its journey could be heard coming but the nearest one dropped to us was at least 200 yards away making a terrific shell crater. We were both glad to get away from that duty.

"I was given eight days leave, all that was allowed at that time, and my father said almost jokingly: "When are they going to make you a corporal?" This had the affect of spurring me on and when I returned I began to work on a plan I had thought out. I had made up my mind I would get promotion."

The way Harry went about getting that promotion showed the sort of character he was. He wasn't satisfied with his rank as a trooper. He wanted to be an NCO. A combination of careful planning, hard work and cunning meant his leadership skills were recognised on August 30, 1916, when he was made a Lance Corporal. After returning to action after his brief hospitalisation with trench foot he volunteered for special courses in a bid to get recognised. Still unable to catch the eye of those in authority he took a different route.

He told how he went about ensuring his face became known so he made the officer ranks:

"The Squadron Sgt Major was continually changing his batman, the man who cleaned his buttons and saddling, and groomed his horses. At the first opportunity I volunteered to take on this job and really tried hard to please him.

"I knew him a little in private life and I heard him say on more than one occasion what a good batman he now had, but I had something else in mind. Although whilst working for him I was excused guards and parades and had a good life as well as 2/6 a week extra - which the Sgt Maj. paid me - after three months I went to him and told him I wished to go back into the ranks.

"He was very surprised and asked me the reason why this was my choice and without hesitation I said that I wasn't satisfied with my rank as a trooper I wanted to become an NCO. It hit home and within a month I was made a Lance Corporal second in command of a section of eight men and eight horses.

"I was supposed to be a good rider and these facts plus the fact that I had two badges for gunnery and signalling meant it was only a few months before I was given my second stripe. I soon gained confidence and although the old sweats used to sing "A Little Child Shall Lead Them" as we marched into the trenches I was quite at ease and was soon making some of them jump to it."

Despite the stories we hear about tanks in the First World War, it was still very much a military campaign where horses were particularly important for transporting supplies and artillery guns. Harry's care for horses back home in Wiltshire came to the fore. He told how he worked with his horse to entertain himself and others:

> "I taught my horse a few tricks. He would always lift his right foot to 'shake hands' when I gave a sharp word of command "shake hands". I could get him to lay down if I said "lay down" and if I touched the inside of his front legs and then the rear legs he would fold his front legs and then his rear legs, finishing up with all four legs under his body.
>
> "But best of all was the trick he played on me. I was standing close to him, near his front legs with my back facing the same way as the horse. I started to rub his tummy when I felt a bang in the right side. He had turned his head and had driven his teeth into my side but he didn't bite me, he didn't close his jaws. I was so relieved I straight away got him a handful of oats. I was reluctant to do it again fearing he might really bite me, but eventually it became one of his tricks. He would throw his ears back turn his head and really force his mouth into my body but never did he bite me.
>
> "There weren't many of my friends willing to take part, their answer was "I'm not letting the bugger bite me". I always gave him a handful of corn after his tricks which many officers came round to see."

One story from the war that Harry's commanding officer recounted years later was of a horseback expedition through the winter weather of Northern France in late 1916 or early 1917. It was a story Harry also told many times. The following account combines two versions he wrote of the story:

> "When the first battle of the Somme started we had shelled the German trenches to such an extent the Germans evacuated and went back some miles. It was then that the Wiltshire Yeomanry as cavalry

were engaged to make contact with the enemy.

"I was sent out on advanced patrol with another chap, a Lance Corporal who we called Pimples; his name was actually Wart. However it was a terribly wet, cold miserable day when Pimples and I went off.

"We were strictly warned to keep our eyes open as it was not exactly known where the Germans were; furthermore they also had their advanced outposts. It was a terrible day, blowing, very cold and raining and I'm afraid I didn't quite realise what a dangerous job we had.

"We had gone some distance and were going up a fairly steep incline in this terrible weather. We reached the top of this incline and then right in front of us was a German outpost - eight to 10 Germans huddled together, crouching down beneath waterproof sheets out of the weather in a sunken road.

"They were obviously trying to keep down out of the elements and had not seen us as we approached otherwise it would have been the end of us both. We were so much taken by surprise we did not know what the hell to do. Pimples galloped away to the right and I turned and went back down the hill like hell for leather.

"As I galloped down the hill I could see the rifle bullets hitting the ground all around me but I got away without injury. How they missed I shall never know. I could see the bullets hitting the ground and with so big a target - two men on horseback.

"Of course I reported immediately to my Troop Commander and then to the Commanding Officer who gave me a severe telling off. I thought I was going to lose my stripe, his point being that if we had retained our presence of mind we could have captured this German outpost unit and of course it was important to take prisoners for information. If they had been doing their job we should both have been picked off like sitting ducks as we approached."

The Commanding Officer, Edward Audry, remembered the incident and wrote to Harry in 1976 when Bristol City Football Club was promoted to the First Division and said that the club's elevation to the top tier of English football would never have happened if the German soldiers had been better marksmen on that day!

On September 26, 1917, maybe just ahead of an engagement, Harry made out a simple Will. Asked who he would like to bequeath his belongings to his first thoughts were for his younger blind brother, who he knew would find it tough in life. The simple Will read: "In the event of my death I give the whole of my property and effects to my brother Arthur Dolman, The Bell Hotel, Yatton Keynell, near Chippenham, Wiltshire."

Harry's overseas service ended on October 18, 1917, and after a month or two back in Blighty in a reserve brigade he was posted to the Officers Cadet Battalion of the Wiltshire Regiment. There was a gruelling four month training course held at Worcester College, Oxford. Harry came out near the top of the squad of 24.

He was proud to put a pip on his shoulder as he was appointed Temporary Second Lieutenant in the Reserve Battalion of the Gloucestershire Regiment at Sittingbourne in Kent. Around that time he was picked for one representative football game for the Aldershot Command football team. This was a prestigious army team and Harry turned out at centre-forward for the representative side.

But for someone interested in engineering, machinery and innovative invention, there was nothing more exciting than the work of the Royal Air Force. Harry was fascinated by the fast growing technology of powered flight. He had been five-years-old when the Wright Brothers had flown for the first time and he had heard all through his childhood exciting tales of how engineers were working on ways for people to take to the skies.

Planes had first been used in the war for aerial reconnaissance with both sides using them to spot movements and map trenches. Harry had seen trench warfare first hand and how little movement there was for months and months as both sides dug in. Tanks had made some breakthroughs but many had got bogged down in the muddy fields of Northern France and Belgium. Many top military minds believed that victory might come from whoever conquered the skies. It is said that it was French air ace Roland Garros who first fixed a machine gun to the front of his plane. The "fighter" aircraft was born and soon France, Britain and Germany were all manufacturing fighter planes. It was pioneering days with inventions and ideas abounding as the war continued.

So it is no surprise that when he heard a call for volunteers to join the Royal Air Force, Harry stepped forward and found himself in Reading at the RAF Instruction School of Aviation where he attended a "Preliminary Course of Instruction In Aviation". After a few months he transferred to the RAF Armaments School in Ealing, London, arriving there on October 19, 1918. He said of those final days of the war:

"The training was a bit lax, leave was easy to obtain and I spent a good deal of time at home and the war was ended before I completed my course. Every man knows what happened on the day peace was declared. We smashed the officers mess completely then dashed off to London and like thousands we got completely drunk. Needless to say I was ill the next day, but it was worth it.

"For months after this we messed about doing nothing and everyone got thoroughly fed up but as I had no job to go to back to I was happy to stay on in the army. Presently we were told to rejoin the units which we had left to go into training for the Flying Corps and I eventually found myself in Yorkshire stationed with the 1st Battalion of the Gloucestershire Regiment at Catterick Camp. I had now grown to love life in the army. Eight applied for a permanent commission. The CO was very sympathetic and lodged my application which I'm sure would have gone through had I not married in September, 1919. I did a PT course at Aldershot and again came out with flying colours and was awarded a first class certificate."

Peacetime had led to changes of plan and the rush to the skies did not seem so important to the military. Decisions had to be made about how best to deploy the troops and on February 27, 1919, a letter was sent to the Armaments School about the future of Harry Dolman.

It read: "Please instruct 2/Lieut. H.J. Dolman to report forthwith to 3rd Gloucester Regiment at Maidstone for duty and inform this office of date he ceases to be employed with Royal Air Force."

So it was back to the army for Harry but his six months in the exciting pioneering world of aviation had sparked a great interest in flying.

Still trying to get further commissions in the army, Harry asked his former head teacher, Mr K. Southgate, to provide a reference from Yatton Keynell School.

It read: "I hereby certify that Harry J. Dolman spent several years in this school of which I am Head teacher under my personal supervision and that I found him very painstaking and industrious in his studies and I feel confident his education is sufficient to justify his advance in the Army and obtain a Commission."

It had been on one of those frequent trips back to Wiltshire that affairs of the heart took over. During a period of leave he met Doris Parnell from Kington Langley in Chippenham. He walked her home and her mother came out to see the suitor off but was so taken with Harry that she invited him in.

Doris was the same age as Harry and their romance developed quickly; on September 2, 1919, they married at a local church. Afterwards the families posed for a wedding photograph outside the door of his father's pub, taking chairs outside. Harry sat in the middle proudly in his uniform, complete with gloves and puttees, with his pretty young bride on his arm holding a bouquet of local flowers.

Everyone is resplendent in their best hats and the bridesmaids and Harry's brother took up a central position with his father, smiling proudly under his bowler.

Although Harry was keen to stay in the army, rules had been made to ensure married men were the first to be released into civilian life.

Just weeks after Harry's wedding a letter was written from the War Office in Whitehall to him and delivered to his parents' pub in Yatton Keynell. It was sent from Sir Bertram Blakston Cubitt, Assistant Under-Secretary of State for War.

He wrote: "Sir, I am commanded by the Army Council to inform you that in consequence of the demobilisation of the Army, a notification will be published in the London Gazette at an early date, to the effect that you relinquish your commission on completion of service as from 11th October 1919.

"You will retain the rank of Second Lieutenant but such retention does not confer the right to wear uniform except on appropriate occasions of a military nature.

"I am to take this opportunity of conveying the thanks of the Army Council for your services during the late war, and for having done all in your power to assist in bringing it to a successful conclusion."

Harry remembers it:

"An army regulation came out banning officers married and under 26 gaining permanent commissions and so my military life came to an end.

"I received my demob papers at Crystal Palace and as I took them I remember glancing at something on the floor which looked like a new farthing. I picked it up and realised immediately it was a half sovereign. I was now a civilian, no job, very little money, little prospect and married with a baby on the way.

"There was a good deal of unemployment. I had only been in the engineering trade a couple of years before the war and when I saw the works manager of Saxby & Farmer Limited he told me there was no chance of my being taken back. It seemed that life did not have much to offer and I lived with my parents for a while at the Bell Inn, Yatton Keynell.

"I would have taken any job to earn a living; in fact I helped my father doing all kinds of farm work. I had my khaki clothes dyed brown. I couldn't afford civvy clothes. Some man had pinched my British overcoat a day or so before I was demobilised and the only other thing I possessed was my old army trench coat and this had to last for a very long time."

Soon Harry moved to Bristol with his young bride to start an engineering course at the Merchant Venturers Technical College. It was a Government scheme to help young army officers and carried a grant of nearly £3 a week, if you were married.

They first moved in with Doris' parents then made their own home in rooms in Bellevue Road, Eastville, not far from the football ground of Bristol Rovers.

The war was over, Harry could concentrate on his passion for machines and inventions and learn his trade. His love of the army life didn't end there though - as he re-enlisted as a Territorial soldier with the rank of Private in the Royal Wiltshire Yeomanry in June 1920, so he was able to do some part-time soldiering alongside his engineering.

He could also continue his passion for football by popping along to watch Bristol Rovers play on a Saturday as it was close to home. Harry, aged 22, may now have been a family man, with responsibilities and a wealth of memories of the war behind him - but he was just starting out on his successful journey.

APPRENTICE TO DIRECTOR

I n the early 1920s cigarettes were a glamorous accessory that every Tommy telling his stories of the Great War had dangling from his lips and every would-be fashionable flapper had placed daintily into a long holder.

Sales were on the increase and Bristol was a major centre of the industry thanks to WD and HO Wills, makers of Wills' Woodbines, the most popular brand with soldiers of the First World War. Millions of cigarettes were being produced in Bristol and thousands of people worked in the factories, which had become increasingly mechanised throughout the industrial revolution.

Many Bristol businesses thrived alongside Wills' by providing the cigarette makers with everything from cellophane and cardboard boxes for packaging to transport and machinery. Getting a good contract with Wills' could mean great success.

One such company was Brecknell, Munro and Rogers, which had roots going back into the previous century. It had been founded by Mr Henry Brecknell as a non-ferrous foundry, originally making things like plumbing brassware and tramway components.

During the war the company had been engaged in making munitions, mainly the production of 18 Pounder HE (high explosive) and shrapnel shells. At that time they had more than 1,000 workers, many of them women.

They also had a culture of modernising equipment and continually inventing new methods to increase production. They boasted that in 1915 a task that took a skilled man 30 minutes to perform in the factory had been so improved through technology that by 1917 a woman could do the same job in 15 seconds.

The company had sites in Lawrence Hill, Jacob Street, St Phillips, Henry Street, Newtown and Thrissell Street, which had been built on the site of an old chapel and cemetery but had expanded to cover around two-and-a-half acres.

As the munitions work ended the company turned to making tobacco machinery, taking over some functions from another local business, Cosmos Engineering, which was already making some machinery for the cigarette industry. Among those working at the business they took over was Frederick George Room, who had received the Victoria Cross in 1917.

Lance Corporal Room was awarded the VC because of his actions on August 16, 1917, at Frezenberg, Belgium, where he had been in charge of a line of stretcher-bearers. He worked continuously under intense fire, dressing the wounded and helping to evacuate them.

His Victoria Cross citation reads: "Throughout this period, with complete disregard for his own life, he showed unremitting devotion to his duties."

Now he was back in the UK quietly working as a lathe operator making machines to be used in the tobacco factories.

It was by pure chance that Harry Dolman joined Brecknell, Munro and Rogers as a Junior Draughtsman in 1921 after finishing his course at the Merchant Venturers Technical College. On the course he had been six months behind everyone else as he had been late joining.

He was working at trying to catch up, attending night school three nights a week. He was making himself ill with so much swotting but was building up his engineering knowledge. When the class closed in 1921 he had only been there 18 months but had been promised two years as part of the Government scheme.

To make up the time he was placed for just six months with Brecknell, Munro and Rogers, where he was expected to complete his studies. His first son, Ron was born in July 1920 so with a wife and toddler at home and only six months of work for certain he was keen to ensure a permanent position.

During this period Harry said farewell to the Royal Wiltshire Yeomanry and received his discharge certificate from the Defence Force on July 4, 1921.

Harry told of those days:

"I was married with a son and unemployment in Bristol was very high. The weeks went by and one day I plucked up the courage to ask the Chief Designer, a Scotsman, what my chances were of staying with the firm.

"I explained that I was married and had a child but to my surprise he said: "You are the best junior draughtsman we have and I would like you to stay on", but he wasn't sure whether the boss would agree as there was a general shortage of work.

"However, a week or so after, I was asked to go to the boss's office. Mr Harry Brecknell, the boss, and the chief designer, were together and I was told to sit down. The boss said: "I have good reports about you and I'm prepared to give you a job at £3 per week".

"I knew it was going to be tough living on this wage but I had no alternative so accepted without argument. - A few weeks later the chief designer was sacked at a minute's notice and there was a general reorganisation and a new chief designer appointed; little did I think at that time that within a few years the chief designer, who was now my immediate boss, would be working under me.

"He was, however, a very competent engineer and designer and taught me a great deal. Furthermore I continued with night school. Later on I begged him to give me some designing to do. I now had a feeling of confidence and ideas came easily to me. I was exceptionally quick with my drawings and was exceptionally good in maths. the latter I put down to the fact that I had bought a second hand maths book for 1/- which I studied almost daily.

"I became so efficient that I could work out problems in my head which the average person would do in twice the time with pencil and paper and it was quite a common occurrence for the senior designers to get me to work out their mathematical problems. It soon became known to the boss and he used my ability frequently. He also introduced me to a local business friend of his who gave me a very difficult mathematical problem connected with his own business for which I was given £5. This indeed was pennies from heaven as I had found it very difficult to live on £3 per week.

"Fortunately my rent for the two unfurnished rooms at 13 Bellevue Road, Eastville, was low - 6/- per week - and to augment my wages I gave up playing football and started refereeing. Mr John Kennedy gave me my referees test. I received anything from 3/- to 5/- for the matches in the Suburban League. I enjoyed every minute and the money enabled me to buy a few cigs every week.

"To augment my wages still further I took on an agency for selling suet. After eating my sandwiches at lunch time I would go off on my bike trying to get orders for suet. I made some earnings but it was hard going and not very remunerative and I was afraid my boss would find out so I packed that spare time job in and asked for a rise, which was granted.

"Holidays were almost out of the question but one year I did spend a week at Weston with my wife and two children. Money was so tight I finished 2/6 short for the week's digs and had to pawn a ring to pay for that and other debts that had accrued."

Brecknell, Munro and Rogers already had a fantastic track record and a good reputation in Bristol before Harry Dolman joined in his junior role. It had made overhead line materials and trolley standards for the electric trams on the Old Market to Kingswood line, going on to sell them to tram companies all over the world.

The tobacco companies were using Standard cigarette making machines, which had been developed by American Machine and Foundry Company (Amfo Co) which set up a UK subsidiary in 1919. Brecknell, Munro & Rogers gained a licence to manufacture the machines in the UK, to save import costs, and had the freedom to make improvements to them along with Imperial Tobacco.

Harry's inventive mind was astonishing, as can be seen from a patent dated October 1922, registered from the rooms he was renting in Bellevue Road. His second son Ray was born in 1921 so at that time he was living in the rooms with Doris and his two young boys. Harry was just 25 years old at that time but the patent is for "Improvements in revolving cylinder internal-combustion engines".

Basically he had invented his own internal combustion engine. The patent lodged included the superb drawings that he did on a board propped up at home showing exactly how it might work. The fact that he not only came up with the invention, was able to draw it and specify it in such detail, and had the presence of mind to apply for the patent demonstrates why he was about to be so successful in his career.

Just in that first patent he showed that he not only had original ideas, but also had a strong eye on how he might make money from his inventions and how he could protect them so that others could not steal his thunder.

This precocious and ambitious attitude got him into big trouble early in his career as a junior draughtsman at Brecknell, Munro and Rogers, as Harry recalled:

"I was little more than a junior draughtsman, in fact I was designing regularly and at this time was doing a lot of development work and design in connection with the cut off on cigarette making machines.

"This particular unit was the limiting factor for speed in the production of cigarettes and I, of course, became an expert with the techniques of this part of the machine. So much so that I could see the failings of the existing design. There were several and in my spare time at home I designed a unit that operated through entirely different principles, the main differences being that whereas all the old machines had worked on reciprocating lines, my new scheme was entirely rotary which enabled this unit to work very much faster.

"It was not long before I had a complete management drawing, which I had done at home after work. I was very pleased with the idea and took the drawing to show my chief designer. He also was very impressed and at once took it down to the boss.

"I'm not quite sure what was in my mind regarding this design other than the fact that I was trying to show my employer that I could design if given the opportunity. I gathered that Mr Brecknell, my boss, was also impressed but strangely enough I just didn't hear any more about the job.

"This hurt somewhat and I mentioned the matters to a friend. His reply was: "Why don't you patent the idea?" I decided to forget all about it for a week or two hoping that the matter would be raised again but such was not the case. Then stupidly, or otherwise, I decided to write to a local tobacco company giving a general outline of my design. They replied suggesting that I should apply for a patent before they saw it. Just about this time the chairman of the company I was engaged by was attending a meeting at the tobacco company's offices and by a fluke the matter came up. The chairman of the company was not impressed that I should have taken such a step in writing to the tobacco company and that evening I was called in to his office and given the sack. Two weeks notice and a severe ticking off.

"I thought this was to end my career as a draughtsman and

with Brecknell, Munro and Rogers. A special board meeting was called to consider the matter. The board consisted of three directors of Brecknell, Munro and Rogers and three from other larger organisations.

"Eventually I was instructed to go to the board room and I expected another ticking off. I had not had any disloyal intentions towards the firm who were paying my wages; neither had I thought of any money gain. I mainly wanted to see an idea of mine developed. In fact I was confident it was a good idea, much better than anything in use, and I had only acted as I did because I thought it was important and nothing had been done.

"When I arrived in the board room feeling very nervous I was told to sit down. In fact everyone was drinking tea and I was invited to have a cup. I was so nervous that I nearly spilt the lot on the carpet. The boss asked why I had approached another firm and I gave him my explanation, stressing that it was really pure pride in the fact that I had produced a brand new method of doing a job in a much better way.

"They explained to me that they had just elaborately tooled up the latest type of unit for doing the same operation and that the company had received a large order for this unit and that if they ever thought of changing over to my new idea it would at the least put a number of people out of work; all these elaborate tools would be scrapped and it would be months before they could get into production on my new idea.

"If I had only been given this information I'm sure I would not have approached the tobacco company but in those days bosses did not take their employees into their confidence as is done today. However, before I left the boardroom I was complimented on my design ability. I was offered a five year contract with the company at a salary triple that I had been receiving. My new idea was never developed but later cut off units were made on a rotary principle which resulted in very much increased speed in the production of cigarettes.

"This was the beginning of a very rapid rise in my status with this company and in the months following I was given many opportunities to encourage my designing ability so much so that I was moved to Pennywell Road and became chief designer of a small drawing office."

Following the pay rise the family moved to a bigger house in the Staple Hill area of Bristol. Harry and Doris named the home Rondray, made up of the name of their two sons, Ron and Ray, with a D for "Dolman" in the middle. Harry's main motivation was to work hard and provide for his growing family.

Throughout the 1920s the drawings flowed from his pen and patents were granted in the UK, throughout Europe and in the USA. Many were improvements to coin-fed apparatus, which were taking off across the world as a mechanised way of selling to the public.

Vending machines meant that chocolate bars and cigarettes could be sold after hours or be placed in unmanned areas on railway stations or places where the public might go at night. They needed to be secure and they needed to be able to identify a real shilling, sixpence, threepenny bit or penny from a dud or foreign coin. It was a completely new area of work and Harry soon became the expert in it. Within months the firm and Harry's name were coupled with many worldwide patents.

By 1927, just six years after joining the firm, Harry was made chief engineer. He was put in charge of a small independent part of the business in Pennywell Road, Bristol, next to the Vestry Cinema (a building it would later take over), concentrating on the design and development of the vending machines. In a major re-organisation the traction side of the business was re-named Brecknell Willis and Co while the Easton Road site was renamed Thrissells.

A year later the firm hit difficulties. Hugh Innes Rogers OBE, who had been crucial in the gaining of the First World War work for the firm, died in October 1928, leaving the business to his son - also called Hugh Rogers. Order books were drying up and a decision was made to re-incorporate the business and split it into three different companies. Hugh Rogers Junior could see that so much of the future success depended on Harry Dolman and the work he was doing in Pennywell Road. Just a month after the death of his father he turned to Harry for help.

Harry takes up the story:

"It was one evening when I was working late designing the ticket issuing machine now so widely known on the underground in London that Mr Hugh Rogers approached me and asked if I would be willing to go partners with him in taking over Brecknell, Munro and Rogers.

"We were a small concern now, independent of the old company. The different managers had not been very successful and the company was heavily in debt, had little business in hand, poor buildings and plant, and liable to go into liquidation any time unless somebody did something quickly.

"Of course I had no money. I had barely been with the company about seven years and I had very little business experience. I didn't like to say I had no money because I thought this would queer my pitch right away. I had plenty of courage and I knew that the company couldn't be run any worse than it had been. Furthermore I was prepared to work with no limit as to how much I did. So my answer was that I would carefully think it over. In fact I had already made up my mind. The capital of the company was £75,000; the debt was in the region of £50,000 and about 80 to 100 people were employed. The price fixed for the sale was £11,000 of which Hugh Rogers and I were to become responsible for £5,000 each. The other £1,000 was divided between two old employees of the company.

"How was I to pay £5,000? I hadn't £5,000. I decided if I took out an insurance policy for £5,000 there was some degree of meeting my responsibility if anything happened to me. That was agreed to and my partners did likewise, the premium of about £86 per annum being paid by the company.

"I became a director of the company together with Hugh Rogers and from then on I was roughly a half owner of BMR 1928 Ltd. It was then, and only then, that I realised what I had taken on. My wife expected me to go to work more and make more a week now I was a director. The old saying came to mind "Be employed and have little money or be the employer and have all the money".

"If I had been a worrying sort I could never have got through but my father had always taught me that hard work would get anybody by, so I just set about the task. The first thing was to find something to make."

Over the next 10 years Harry proved to be a shrewd and successful businessman. The business that he was running in Pennywell Road, Bristol, expanded to take over the Vestry Cinema next door as he found ways to expand the vending machine business and diversify into other machines.

Harry held the patents to the vending machines that were now being sold across the world. The Underground Railway Authorities in London saw the advantages of automatic vending. It meant people could buy tickets themselves from machines rather than having to have manned ticket sales booths. In London, where thousands of people needed to move swiftly around on the tube system every day, it could prove a massive saving. It was Harry that was coming up with the ways to enable people to buy tickets cheaply from a machine and then pass through a turnstile gate using that ticket. Trains could board faster, people could get around easier and there was less queueing at manned booths and gates.

The string of inventions was getting Britain's capital city moving and Britain's consumers were getting used to the idea that they could pop out for a packet of fags or a chocolate bar at any time of the day - even when the shops were closed. It increased sales and was a huge advantage for the public.

Of course others, particularly in Germany, were coming up with rival systems, but Brecknell's succeeded in becoming the main contractor for the London Transport ticket machine requirements. Harry was forward-thinking and realised that the company needed to demonstrate its expertise on the world stage. He decided that the vending machines needed a worldwide shop window and took the decision to exhibit them at the 1929 International Exposition, which was being held in Barcelona.

The Exposition, which ran from May 20, 1929, until January 15, 1930, was a massive event attended by more than 200,000 visitors from across the world and was a celebration of technological advances.

Many people had their homes relocated in Barcelona to make way for the buildings that housed the displays; public buildings that still stand today were created and transport links, public lighting, a tram system and sewerage network were installed that are still being used today.

Innovations were on display from 20 European countries and some private organisations from the USA and Japan. The vending machines invented by Harry Dolman caused a sensation and scooped a gold medal. To win the top award for vending machines at such a significant global event was a massive achievement for the firm and put Harry Dolman on the world map.

The year 1929 also saw the completion of his family with the birth of his fourth child, Hazel. Harry's eldest son Ron was, by then, 10-years-old; second son Ray was two years younger; daughter Frances, always known as Frankie, had been born in 1925 and Hazel completed the family.

With four children under 10 years old, Doris had her hands full at home but Harry's inventions were now bringing good rewards. The family moved to a bigger house in Church Road, Staple Hill. The builder of the estate had reserved this larger house for his own family, so it was plenty big enough to house the growing Dolman family and had a garage, where Harry set up his own lathe and drawing boards, so he could continue his work at home.

The optimism of the international exposition in Barcelona was reflected in the mood at Brecknell, Munro and Rogers in the years following. Bristol had a lot of engineering companies and Harry Dolman wanted the best working for him - so he set up an apprentice scheme in a bid to ensure the best young brains came to his firm.

He also turned his mind to machines that might be used for leisure and pleasure and from the early 1930s came up with one-armed bandits with names such as Aeroplay, The Brooklands Racer and Football Shooter to reflect the growing interest in flying, racing cars and football.

Harry held the patent for these machines, although many of the ideas came from those who worked for him. Soon the business was boasting of being the largest manufacturer of coin-operated machines in the UK.

But Harry had not forgotten his rural roots and alongside the vending machines and coin-slot games he started looking at a way to mechanise the grading of eggs, a difficult task, handling the most delicate of products. An egg grading machine that he patented in May 1930 was to be the next major success. He tells the story of those first years in business:

"We had been experimenting with an idea of mine for grading eggs so I really got my head down on the drawing board and in a few weeks the first egg grader left our work to go into service in an egg packing station in Hungerford. I won't dwell on the teething troubles but there were plenty which I attended to myself and one of our distributors gave us an order for 50 machines. This was indeed a good start off but 50 machines at about £90 each didn't take us far.

"I was prepared to design anything providing there was a future and by chance I was told there was a market for a machine which could compete with the fruit machines imported from the States, a gambling machine, illegal in England. However I was offered an order for 500 providing it would keep clear of the American patents and give satisfaction. Again I set about the job and produced a machine known as The Racer and I honestly believe this saved Brecknell's. We sold a large number and whilst I hated this line of business, we had to live. We made a number of other amusement machines and then started a retail sales organisation.

"I designed the ticket issuing machine and although we were up against very keen competition from the Germans we succeeded in obtaining quite a substantial order from the London Underground. We only succeeded after a lot of teething troubles and headaches. On more than one occasion I remained at work in the factory on the drawing board for 48 hours, sometimes more.

"Our retail sales were now getting business for vending machines and the egg grader was selling slowly and at the end of the first year we only showed a loss of £5,000 with a turnover of about £65,000. From then on we never looked back.

"My partner and I each received very small salaries and all profit made was ploughed back into the business. We had a heavy debt to pay off and that was our first aim and object. We also had to buy new plant; the machines we possessed were worn out, inaccurate, and slow. We had a few employees who had never worked elsewhere other than Brecknells and our factory was a home from home for many of them.

"My partner, Hugh Rogers, had recently left Cambridge University and was terribly keen. Like his father, he had an excellent business technique. His first class education made up for something I did not possess. My only criticism of him was that he would not take chances, a thing you must do in business.

"However, we worked together for about 12 years and never had a serious disagreement. We had lots of arguments on detail which resulted for the good of the company. He wrote business letters which I had nothing but admiration for and when he left in 1948 to take up an appointment with the Ministry of Supply I endeavoured to emulate his style in letter writing. I learnt a lot from him in the 12 years we were together."

Harry had secured a European patent for the egg grading machine under the heading "improvements in apparatus for sorting articles according to weight". It worked by the eggs being fed mechanically or manually into a series of weigh-pans that discharged their contents into compartments.

Harry's ingenious drawings and description of the various counterweights, fulcrums, flanges, brackets and supporting bars that enabled eggs to be sorted into different sizes were impressive. The machine was a major time saver and therefore money-earner for the dairy industry and once again Brecknell, Munro and Rogers achieved a gold medal - this time at the British Dairy Farmers Association show held at Olympia, London, in 1931. The device was further improved and in 1935 won a silver medal at the Royal Ulster

Agricultural Show.

In fact Harry had worked out a way to ensure that his machines could always be improved and developed. Customers would buy the machines and have them on their premises. Engineers would then be able to make improvements to them constantly and the improvements would then be incorporated into the next generation of machines.

This technique continued for decades. Derek Andrews, who worked for Brecknells from 1957, said: "The egg grading machines were constantly being improved and developed and we managed to get speeds up from testing 10,000 eggs an hour to 12,800 eggs an hour by going out in the field.

"To really test the machines you had to have thousands of eggs of different shapes and sizes and there was no way that an engineering company could acquire such things. Harry would sell a machine cheaply to someone and then we would develop it from there. In my time the machines got more and more sophisticated with different tests, handling and packaging systems."

Back in the 1930s all the international success meant that Harry was a wealthy man. He moved from smoking cigarettes to cigars and he was able to afford his own car and ensure his wife and children had all the home comforts. It wasn't all plain sailing though as one of the early drivers of a private car on Bristol's roads.

In July 1933 he was driving along Stapleton Road, not far from his home, and had an accident that landed him in court.

The report of the case at the time says: "Defendant says as he approached the junction, at about 20 miles an hour, he passed a motor-cycle combination, and then noticed the cyclist about three yards away. The cyclist put out his hand, and then started to turn. Witness swerved in an endeavour to avoid the cyclist."

There was a collision and Harry was fined £3 and ordered to pay

£1 10s costs, at Bristol Police Court, for driving a motor car without due care and attention.

The minor setback didn't put Harry off the excitement of owning his own vehicle. He was happy to tell everyone in the family at the time that he had three ambitions in life; to own his own company, to own a Rolls Royce and to get a knighthood. The cars were getting bigger and better every time he purchased a new one and his earnings meant he was well on the way to his first Rolls Royce. He already had his name linked to an internationally successful business and his inventions and entrepreneurship were attracting the interest of the Government.

But Harry was not content to trundle around the Bristol roads avoiding cyclists - he had been bitten by the flying bug in the last days of the First World War. He had been partially through his pilot training when peace was signed and had been looking forward to operating a flying machine. Surely, the future would see everyone have their own private plane - and naturally Harry wanted to be the first to have one.

THE FLYING FLEA

Hazel Dolman was just seven years old when her father, who had excitedly been reading a book full of instructions and drawings for a number of days, took over the main living room of the family's detached house in Church Road, Staple Hill, Bristol, as a workshop.

She said: "He said he was building a plane. Some of the work went on in the garden but every night he was busy in the main living room and pretty soon the fuselage took shape and we had a little single-seater aeroplane, apart from the wings, sitting inside the house.

"The problem was it would no longer go out through the door. That didn't seem to bother him though. He just arranged for some people to come around and take the entire window frame out so that it could be lifted out that way. It was an exciting day when the plane was lifted through the gap where the window was and was plonked on the driveway. I don't think my mother was terribly impressed, but it was pretty typical of my father. If he was determined to do something he would find a way to do it."

The little plane that Harry had built was a Flying Flea. He had read about it in the newspaper and decided he wanted to build one. He sent off for the handbook in 1936 and his adventure began. It was dubbed the "smallest practical aeroplane in the world" in its publicity material and the media said it "may well be the motorcycle of the future".

Officially called the Mignet H.M 14 Pou du Ciel the Flying Flea was a single-seat tandem-wing ultra light aircraft that had been designed by a Frenchman, Henri Mignet. It was introduced to the world in 1934 by Mignet, who had set about designing a plane that could be built by the "man-in-the-street" in his garage, attic, or in Harry's case, the living room.

The Illustrated London News of August 1935 carried a whole page about it under the headline: "Will this be the aeroplane for the million?" The idea was that everyone with more than basic engineering and DIY skills would be able to build their own aeroplane to travel around in. Harry certainly had the requisite skills, money and enthusiasm and it seemed that it was meant for him!

The Illustrated London News article said: "M. Henri Mignet has evolved and constructed a very remarkable little aeroplane called the Flying Flea, which, being easy to build, is receiving considerable attention. No fewer than 400 amateurs in France are busy making their own 'planes of this type, and, also, a number are under construction in England, where M. Mignet recently arrived to give demonstration flights.

"He crossed the Channel from St Inglevert to Lympne, in his own Flying Flea in 52 minutes. The Flying Flea is so simply designed that any amateur carpenter can build it, and now numerous firms in this country are supplying the "bits and pieces" all ready for assembly. For instance Messrs. Perman and Co, who are at present building two of these machines, are prepared to supply all the necessary wood cut to shape and marked, all the metal fittings, wheels and tyres, elastic cord, fabric, nails, glue and screws for about £30; so that all one has to do is assemble.

"The engine and air-screw (new) cost another £45 to £60. Naturally, if one cares to fashion the wood and make the fittings oneself, the cost is very considerably less. The fact remains that here is a little aeroplane, built on very simple and revolutionary lines, which, it is claimed, is both easy and safe to fly, and brings flying within the means of thousands of young men in this country."

The article was accompanied by illustrations showing just how simple and easy it was to construct your own Pou du ciel (Louse of the Sky) aeroplane and how an English instruction manual could be obtained from the Air League of the British Empire in Berkeley Street, London.

That was the book that Hazel had seen her father enthusiastically reading after sending away for it. The Daily Express had given major publicity to the plane by following the construction of the first one to be licensed in the UK (G-ADMH), which was built by Stephen Appleby, a friend of the inventor Mignet.

It flew for the first time in July 1935 and was given an airworthiness certificate by the Air Ministry. The next day - July 25, 1935, he demonstrated it to the press, but had to make a forced landing in a ploughed field nearby, where it landed upside down. Appleby said some modifications were needed to the plane and the Daily Express, keen to keep the exciting story running, paid £100 for the modifications.

These included increasing the wing span from five metres to six metres and changing the engine. By December 1935 Appleby was able to pilot the plane from Lympne Airport to St Inglevert Airfield in France - the reverse English Channel crossing to the one his friend Mignet had made to introduce the plane to the UK.

The saga captured Harry's imagination. Even the modifications and changes excited him - after all he was an inventor, a man who liked to come up with modifications to machines. As a wealthy and successful man he also felt that he should be among the first to be piloting his own plane around the country - and maybe even abroad to some of the trade shows and customers that Brecknells had across Europe. Mignet had boasted that his original trip from France to Britain had cost him just two shillings in fuel - a real budget airline!

Mignet had reasoned that conventional flying controls were too complicated so had simplified the mechanisms, doing away with any foot controls. The HM 14 had a pivotal upper mainplane which tilted fore and aft for longitudinal control. The wing had no ailerons and turns were carried out by the means of a very large rudder.

Depending on the engine selected it cost around £700 in parts to build, well within Harry's means. He was looking forward to travelling at 60 mph at heights of up to 6,000 feet and able to cover distances of around 190 miles without refuelling - all boasts made in the instruction manual.

Harry's Flying Flea was one of less than 100 British-built such planes to be granted Permits to Fly. His was given the number G-AEHM and he proudly painted it on the fuselage he had carefully constructed in the living room and in massive letters on the top of the wings that were attached after it had been lifted out through the window.

He proudly named the plane 'Blue Finch' and decorated the tail with a finch in flight. On the cockpit, he wrote his initials in his own registration "HJD 1" optimistically believing that this might just be the first of the private planes he was about to construct for himself.

He was granted permission to fly from Whitchurch Aerodrome in Bristol and transported the plane there on May 4, 1936. Harry, resplendent in a flying helmet, carried out all the last minute checks.

He was particularly keen to make sure that the 35 horse power ABC Scorpion engine, which he had specially selected to power his personalised flying machine, was in tip-top shape. As the last minute checks were being carried out local schoolboys gathered to climb on the nearby picket fence and watch the contraption take to the skies.

Harry spun the propellor and got the engine ticking over just right, hopped into the open cockpit wearing a tweed jacket, shirt and tie and beamed with joy - the pleasure of having made his own aeroplane obvious to all who had gathered to watch the event.

Blue Finch hurtled along the grass at Whitchurch Aerodrome; Blue Finch lifted off the ground and soared to a height of 20 feet then plummeted back to earth, hitting the ground before flipping upside down and coming to rest. Everyone rushed towards the stricken plane only to see Harry still beaming climb unscathed from the cockpit.

But Blue Finch was damaged and needed repairs. It was back to the drawing board for Harry. But, of course the drawing board was a place he felt very comfortable and it wasn't long before he was back at Whitchurch Aerodrome again for another attempt.

In a short account of the Flying Flea, written many years later, Harry described the attempts:

> "I asked permission to fly it at Whitchurch Aerodrome, and after a lot of struggling managed to get it off the ground a few times. On one occasion the oil pipe broke and the oil came out of the engine all over my face.
>
> "I broke a propellor every time I got off the ground. Propellors cost me six guineas a time. On one occasion I landed upside down. I crawled out unhurt, but the ambulance and fire engine came chasing across the aerodrome in case there was a fire and a serious accident to me. The manager of the aerodrome told me: "Take the bloody thing away, Harry, before you kill yourself".
>
> "I then started flying, or hopping would be a better term, at the Hullavington aerodrome in Wiltshire, which was being prepared for the RAF."

In fact Harry had a very lucky escape with his self-build aeroplane. On the day he tried his out for the very first time - May 4, 1936 - pilot Ambrose Cowell crashed a similar Flying Flea (G- AEEW) at

Penshurst Airfield in Kent. He died from his injuries.

The authorities started looking into the issue and found that four other fatal crashes had occurred since August the previous year in France. Just a few weeks later Flying Flea (G-AEBS) crashed at RAF Digby, killing distinguished and skilful pilot Squadron Leader Charles Davidson.

The RAF Officer, who was a World War 1 flying ace in the Royal Flying Corps and RAF, had made the Flying Flea himself in the air station workshops. Questions were now being asked about the safety of this revolutionary plane championed by the Daily Express.

A full scale investigation was launched and it was found that in total 11 people had been killed when their home-made planes had hit the ground in a nose dive. In August 1936 a Flying Flea was mounted in the Air Ministry's wind tunnel at Farnborough for tests requested by the Air League of the British Empire, who were giving the permits to fly. Wind tunnel tests were also carried out in France by the French Air Ministry.

The results of the wind tunnel tests were damning. It was found that at nose-down angles of incidence steeper than 15 degrees, with the joystick hard back, there was insufficient pitching movement to raise the nose. This resulted in a nose-dive from which it was impossible to recover.

With so many fatalities reported and people like Harry finding the Flying Flea impossible to control, the plane that was going to bring flying to the masses was banned. It is understood that 118 Flying Fleas were built in Britain with Harry's just one of 83 to receive permits to fly.

Mignet modified and updated his design, making later aircraft safer, but the public had lost confidence in it and only a handful were later licensed for flight in the UK.

Harry said:

"I read in the paper that these machines were fundamentally unsafe as one had been tested in an air tunnel, and a notice was sent out to all people who had built Flying Fleas not to risk their lives in them.

"So I wrote to the Bristol Museum and asked them if they would like it. They replied they would very much like to have it but that they unfortunately did not have room and suggested that I contact the Kensington Museum, which I did. The machine was duly sent off, complete with a slightly broken propellor."

So, in September 1938, just over two years after Harry sent away for the manual and commandeered the living room to build his own plane, Harry donated the plane to the Science Museum in Kensington, London.

During the Second World War the plane was stored, but saw the light of day again in July 1951 when the Daily Express held a "50 Years of Flying" exhibition in Hendon and put it on display.

Harry's Flying Flea was then stored in Byfleet, before being transferred to the Science Museum's store in Hayes, Middlesex, in 1972. In 1982 it was moved again to Wroughton, in Wiltshire, joining many other exhibits as part of the Science Museum's Aeronautical collection. There restoration work was carried out on it by Stan Wichall, ensuring that it survived to today.

In 2011 the Flying Flea returned to Bristol and is now part of a collection at M Shed, the city's museum that celebrates the people of Bristol, where it is preserved for future generations to see.

WAR, PEACE AND FOOTBALL

Harry Dolman was a wealthy man through the 1930s. His business was doing well. His family was enjoying the fruits of his labour, innovations and ideas, and was living in a nice large house with the children going to good schools.

The money he spent on trying to build his own aeroplane was hardly significant to him. When some business needed to be done in the USA for Brecknell, Munro and Rogers he arranged for his father to move in to the family home to look after the children while he and Doris took a cruise to New York and back.

They travelled over on the *Queen Mary*, which had only been launched in 1936 and was the flagship of the Cunard line, offering the ultimate in luxury travel with its sumptuous art deco design.

It had won the Blue Riband for the fastest crossing of the Atlantic. But the French built ss *Normandie* was said by many to be better and the two ships were competing on the voyage to be the fastest, with the ultramodern ss *Normandie* winning back the Blue Riband after getting some mechanical modifications.

Of course the battle to build the biggest and best cruise liner fascinated Harry so he decided to take the ss *Normandie* on the return trip, so he could compare the two. The ss *Normandie* was a year older than the *Queen Mary* but it had set records both westbound and eastbound across the Atlantic.

Its design was sumptuous and Harry sat proudly on deck with Doris puffing on a cigar enjoying being whisked back across the Atlantic on a ship many gave the title of the "greatest liner ever".

Combining business with pleasure was a familiar theme for many Bristol businessmen and football was increasingly one way that those with a little spare cash liked to indulge. Harry had taken an interest in the non-league football scene. Brecknells had a team and Harry had turned out for them over the years. He also had his refereeing badges so had officiated in many local games. Of course as a local businessman he had also been roped into helping out with some of the organisation of local leagues.

But the decade saw him pass his 40th birthday in 1938 and as the year approached he found himself watching the game more than playing or officiating and he held two season tickets at Bristol Rovers' Eastville Stadium, where he got to know many of those who ran the club.

Among those was Captain Albert James Prince-Cox, a colourful figure just a few years younger than Harry who shared his interest in flying, football and big cigars.

Prince-Cox had served as a pilot in the Royal Flying Corps and was a Fellow of the Royal Meteorological Society and at one time had been employed to deliver the daily weather forecast to the Royal Family at Buckingham Palace. But on Saturday afternoons his passion was football.

He hadn't been much of a player but he became one of England's foremost referees taking charge of 32 internationals in 15 different countries until knee injury forced him to retire as a referee and in 1930 he applied for the job as manager of Bristol Rovers.

He turned up for the interview in a red open-topped sports car smoking a large cigar and over the following few years transformed the team with his flamboyant style. He introduced blue and white quartered shirts to "make the players look bigger and more robust"; he arranged a friendly against the Holland national team, which the Rovers duly won, and he introduced a new nickname for the team - The Pirates.

In 1935, with Eastville attracting big crowds to games, he had called upon Harry to come up with a successful turnstile checker to count the numbers of people getting into the ground. Harry invented a turnstile suitable for the job, patented it, and oversaw its installation at Eastville Stadium.

But in October 1936, just eight months into a new five year contract as manager, Prince-Cox quit the job, saying he wanted to concentrate on promoting boxing, circuses and variety shows. He left on good terms and Harry Dolman was not alone in keeping in touch with the flamboyant figure.

It was inevitable that Harry would be asked if he'd like to join the board of Bristol Rovers and he went along enthusiastically to a couple of meetings to see what being the director of a football club might entail.

He attended two meetings but was disappointed to find that the main topic of conversation seemed to be over plans to sell the Eastville Stadium to the greyhound company, who operated the dog track around the pitch.

Harry's daughter Hazel remembered: "My father always said that it was impossible to make money out of the entrance fees alone in football and the key to a successful club was to make money from the stadium as well.

"He saw the ideas of the Bristol Rovers board in the late 1930s as a backward step and he didn't want to be part of that and so turned down the chance to be on the board. Interestingly it was me and my sister Frances that used to enjoy going with him to football - our brothers weren't very interested in football."

It was former Rovers manager Prince-Cox who suggested that Harry should meet up with Bristol City chairman George Jenkins, who he believed shared his views on how football could be made to pay its way. Prince-Cox arranged the meeting between the two men. Harry tells the story:

"When I joined the board in 1939 I was 42. I was still playing football fairly regularly but I knew I should soon have to give up and I wanted to retain contact with the game. I was at the time a season ticket holder with Bristol Rovers having had two tickets for three or four years, so my interest was in that direction.

"I was invited to attend a board meeting, which I enjoyed very much, and I was asked to come again when all directors would be present. To my great surprise they were in the middle of negotiations to sell the ground in order to get out of debt. Nothing was said about me joining the board. Time was taken up discussing the sale of the premises lock, stock and barrel.

"When I left the ground after the meeting I quite by chance ran into Prince Cox an ex manager of the Rovers and an ex referee. We had been friends for some time by virtue of the fact I financed one of his boxing shows. He persuaded me to go on the City board and suggested that we should go and see the chairman straight away. George Jenkins, the chairman at that time was delighted and at the next meeting I was elected."

Bristol City had enjoyed a good season in 1937/38, which saw Millwall just pip them to the Division 3 (South) title by one point. City finished on 55 points and Millwall on 56. Rovers were in the same division but had finished 15th.

The next season ended with Bristol City slipping to eighth in a league table that saw Bristol Rovers finish bottom of the league. George Jenkins had been persuasive and convinced Harry Dolman that Bristol City were heading for the higher leagues and he was proud to join the board at the end of that season at a meeting held in the Provident Hall, Prewett Street, Bristol.

Of course football is very different to running a private business. Everyone has an opinion and is not afraid to voice it, as many players, managers and directors of clubs find these days on internet forums and social media. Things were not much different in 1939 and Harry got a little taste of what it was like to be in the football spotlight almost immediately.

The Bristol Evening Post had a regular sporting diary column called "World of Sport" written anonymously under the name of "The Traveller" which took a cynical and humorous look at sport. The Traveller duly wrote about Harry's appointment on July 21.

"The Bristol City FC board of directorate is now at full strength. This has been brought about by the appointment of Messrs Arthur Sperring and Harry Dolman as directors.

"When I sat next to him at the recent annual dinner of the Bristol and District Football League not for a single moment did I think that the next time that I spoke to Mr Dolman he would be a director of the Ashton Gate club. That however has happened.

"His first impressions are that the City have got together a really sound side for next season. We have heard that one often enough before and anyway what would you expect a newly-appointed director to say? But Harry has good reasons for saying that, and if those reasons turn out to be well founded everyone will be pleased. "Bristol" said Mr Dolman "with a population of nearly half a million should be able to support at least one club in the upper circle and I have every reason to think the City will get that honour".

"Interesting sidelight on his business is that he personally invented the ticket and change machines on London's underground system. On the Rovers ground at Eastville four seasons back he superintended the installation of a new turnstile checker which he had himself devised and patented,

"He is keenly looking forward to travelling with the club on their out-of-town trips, but before the season starts, he is going away for a three weeks' holiday to Brighton and later to Cornwall.

"It was my pleasure to meet Mr Dolman in the local amateur soccer world nearly 20 years ago. At that time he and I were closely associated with the Bristol and Suburban League. He was the Hon Secretary of the Venturers AFC, members of the Fifth Division of that league and a representative of that club on the league's committee. Mr Dolman therefore, has had a considerable experience in the Soccer world."

In just a few paragraphs The Traveller had painted a nice little pen picture of the typical football director, able to take three weeks holiday, giving the usual platitudes about the team and with little real experience of football at the top level. To round it off nicely "The Traveller" had revealed Harry's previous association with rivals Bristol Rovers - a robust start to living life more in the media spotlight, which Harry was able to laugh off.

But Harry found that once in the board room the finances of football were very different from those of his own successful business and it soon became obvious that he was regarded as much as a source of finance as a management expert. He recalled:

"It was now the end of the 1938/39 season and board meetings were held at least once a fortnight. Like most clubs in the 3rd Division the City were badly in debt, how much was difficult to say, because this was kept secret. Money was owing on several transfer fees and most of the weekly bills were left unpaid. In fact there was always difficulty in finding wages for the players. Almost invariably a threatening letter was received from local tradesmen demanding settlement of their account and I was continually being asked to pay or help to pay."

However it was events across Europe that were dominating everyone's thoughts and they were to mean that Harry Dolman had to put his football management ambitions on the back burner.

Charlie and Ann Dolman pictured in 1913 with their seven children. Back standing, left to right, are: Kate, Jack and Laura; sat middle row, flanking Dad and Mum, are Charles on the left and Harry on the right; sat on the ground, left to right, are Arthur and Victor.

SAXBY & FARMER Ltd.

Chief Offices:—53, VICTORIA STREET, LONDON, S.W.   Works:—CHIPPENHAM, WILTS.

Railway Signals & Safety Appliances.

BLACK'S IMPROVED ECONOMICAL FACING POINT LOCK.

GOLD MEDALS AND HIGHEST AWARDS:

PARIS, 1867, 1876, 1878, 1879, 1881, and 1885; VIENNA, 1873; BRUSSELS, 1876 and 1888; LONDON, 1882, 1885, and 1892; PHILADELPHIA, 1876; MELBOURNE, 1880; ANTWERP, 1885; BARCELONA, 1888; EDINBURGH, 1890; NIJNI-NOVGOROD, 1896; SOUTH AFRICA, 1899; BUENOS AIRES, 1910.

SIGNAL WORK OF EVERY DESCRIPTION, ELECTRICAL & MECHANICAL.

Telephone: 285, Westminster.   Registered Telegraphic Address: "SIGNALMEN, LONDON."

SAXBY & FARMER'S
Munition Workers,
MILLING SEC:.

Top image shows Saxby and Farmer Ltd's Chippenham premises, where Harry worked on railway engineering projects. The photograph was taken from the top of St Paul's Church spire, by Thomas Haywood, an apprentice who went on to became chief draughtsman of the company. Middle image is a Saxby & Farmer advertisement from 1911, and the bottom picture shows the Milling Section during the First World War, when many of Harry's colleagues were engaged in making artillery shells while the likes of Harry and other employees joined the military.

Top: The Royal Wiltshire Yeomanry assembling on horseback in the Market Place, Chippenham, either just before or early in the First World War. Bottom left: Harry proudly wearing his uniform at a Yeomanry territorial camp pre-First World War. Bottom right: Harry on his horse, dressed in full military kit, ready for the Western Front.

Harry pictured in the kit of the Aldershot Command football team in 1918. This was a prestigious army team and Harry played centre-forward for the representative side on one occasion.

Harry, standing back right, and one of the six-a-side football teams put out by Yatton Keynell FC during a tournament played on a field lent by Hulands (Harry's former employer) on Easter Monday 1922.

The marriage of Doris Parnell and Harry Dolman on September 2, 1919. Everyone is resplendent in their best hats and the bridesmaids and Harry's brother took up a central position, with his father smiling proudly under his bowler. Picture taken in front of The Bell public house at Yatton Keynell, run by Charlie Dolman.

PATENT SPECIFICATION 204,914

Application Date: Oct. 14, 1922. No. 27,888 / 22.

Complete Accepted: Oct. 11, 1923.

COMPLETE SPECIFICATION.

Improvements in Revolving Cylinder Internal-combustion Engines.

I, HENRY JAMES DOLMAN, of No. 13, Belle Vue Road, Eastville, Bristol, in the County of Gloucester, a subject of the King of Great Britain & Ireland, do 5 hereby declare the nature of this invention and in what manner the same is to be performed, to be particularly described and ascertained in and by the following statement:—

3 & 4 show the special valve necessary for converting the two-stroke into the four-stroke revolving cylinder engine. 50 Fig. 5 shows the silencer attached to silencer flanged ring.

In the five figures similar parts are marked with like letters of reference.

DESCRIPTION.

Top: the Merchant Venturers College in Unity Street, Bristol, where Harry studied draughtsmanship and engineering. Middle: official notification of Harry's first invention when aged just 25. Bottom: Belle Vue Road, Easton, Bristol, where Harry and his young family rented rooms at number 13, when he first worked for Brecknell, Munro and Rogers (BMR).

Top: BMRs factory in Easton Road, Bristol, pictured in the early 1900s and before the site became part of Thrissell Engineering. Below: some of BMRs engineering products from its Thrissell Street site on display.

Some of BMRs cigarette vending machines featuring Harry's inventions. These were popular with newsagents like H Evans, whose shopfront is seen here in early 1927. The slogan on the vending machine reads, "Why go without a smoke, cigarettes can be obtained from Evan's Automatic Machine after closing hours, the machine is always in use as it is tested every day".

Top: a Bristol City Council publicity shot showing part of the apparatus for one of Harry's egg grading machines. Bottom left: a restored Brooklands Racer penny amusement machine. Bottom right: long before electronic self-service petrol pumps were in common use, Brecknell's had already developed a mechanical version of its own.

WILL THIS BE THE AEROPLANE FOR THE MILLION? THE "FLYING FLEA."

Drawn by our Special Artist, G. H. Davis, from Information Supplied by the Air League of the British Empire and Messrs. E. G. Perman and Co., 24, Brownlow Mews, W.C.1.

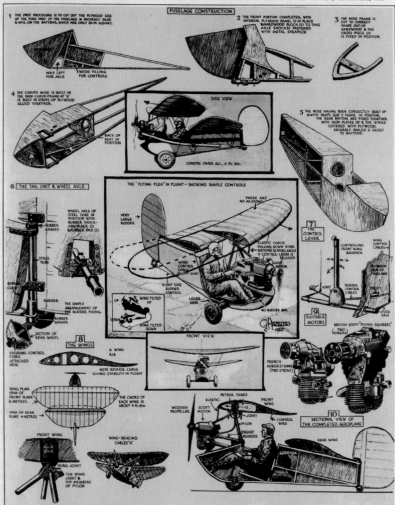

THE "FLYING FLEA" AND ITS COMPONENT PARTS : A SIMPLE LITTLE AIRCRAFT THAT ANY AMATEUR CARPENTER CAN BUILD.

A Frenchman, M. Henri Mignet, has evolved and constructed a very remarkable little aeroplane called the "Flying Flea," which, being easy to build, is receiving considerable attention. No fewer than 400 amateurs in France are busy making their own 'planes of this type, and, also, a number are under construction in England, where M. Mignet recently arrived to give demonstration flights. He crossed the Channel, from St. Inglevert to Lympne, in his own "Flying Flea," in 52 minutes. The "Flying Flea" is so simply designed that any amateur carpenter can build it, and now numerous firms in this country are supplying the "bits and pieces" all ready for assembly. For instance, Messrs. Perman and Co., who are at present building two of these machines, are prepared to supply all the necessary wood cut to shape and marked, and all the metal fittings, wheels and

tyres, elastic cord, fabric, nails, glue, and screws for about £30; so that all one has to do is to assemble. The engine and air-screw (new) cost another £45 to £60. Naturally, if one cares to fashion the wood and make the fittings oneself, the cost is very considerably less. The fact remains that here is a little aeroplane, built on very simple and revolutionary lines, which, it is claimed, is both easy and safe to fly, and brings flying within the means of thousands of young men in this country. In these illustrations we have only attempted to give some idea of how simple is the construction of the "Pou du Ciel," as it is called in French. M. Mignet's book giving full details how to construct this little flying machine has now been translated into English and can be purchased from the translators, the Air League of the British Empire, 19, Berkeley Street, W.1.

Harry's Flying Flea, 'Blue Finch', being assembled at Brecknell's factory.

Bristol Airport at Whitchurch where Harry first tried to fly the plane.

Harry in Blue Finch HJD1 on the 'runway' at Bristol Airport – looking very pleased with himself and resplendent in shirt, tie and jacket.

Harry, second from the right, still looking pleased with himself, and none the worse for wear, having flipped his Flying Flea!

VISIT OF H.M. QUEEN MARY TO
BRECKNELL. MUNRO & ROGERS (1928) LTD
ON JANUARY 13TH 1942.

The visit of Queen Mary to Brecknell, Munro and Rogers during the Second World War on January 13, 1942. Harry achieved the Royal visit by writing a letter to Badminton House where the Queen was staying.

Harry formed a Home Guard unit at Brecknell's during the Second World War and employees in overalls and some men in uniform – including Harry looking at the camera, bottom right – are shown clambering over an old tank at the factory.

Harry, second left, with other Brecknell's Home Guard men, wearing their uniforms with pride.

Late 1940s and Harry is still turning out for the Brecknell's works team, top middle, holding the football, and when he's not playing he's still involved in running the teams, top left in bottom image.

The optimism of the Barcelona Exposition just 10 years before where the hostilities and horrors of the Great War had been put aside and where German engineers had exhibited alongside those of Brecknell, Munro and Rogers had disappeared. Adolf Hitler was Chancellor of Germany and Nazi soldiers were on the streets of Poland.

On September 3, 1939, Britain declared war on Germany and, although the football season kicked off as planned, it was soon abandoned, as the more important matter of fighting a World War took precedence.

One person that really impressed Harry Dolman at this time was Winston Churchill. Harry loved Churchill's leadership and he liked his style, telling many of his close friends and family in later years that he modelled his own image of being seen in a good hat and smoking a fat cigar on the wartime leader that came to the fore with his rousing speeches and bulldog spirit.

For Brecknell, Munro and Rogers it was another change of direction as the firm had to find relevant work during the war while many of its employees went off to fight. Harry found himself in sole charge after his business partner Hugh Rogers took a Government post in the Ministry of Food as part of the war effort. Although now in his 40s, Harry was keen to do his bit. He described the war years in business:

"When the war broke out I was torn between staying with Brecknells and joining up. In the end I decided to join up. I had had over five years' military experience in the First World War. I was as fit as a young man of 20 and I felt sure I could do work in the services so off I went, had my medical and waited to be posted. Meanwhile Rogers was offered the important appointment with the Ministry which I could tell he was very keen to take. I therefore gave way and our partnership ended, neither of us knew how long for and what the future had in store for us.

"I now found myself the boss of Brecknells. There was a war on and we were producing things which were useless to the war effort and our sales had rapidly declined. We still had a comparatively poor plant and not very extensive premises and poor fixtures. Our fitters were leaving us to take up employment with well-established war provision firms. In the past 10 years we had not only cleared our debt but had been paying ourselves substantial dividends and the very successful business which we had built up suddenly looked as though it might fade to next to nothing.

"The profit dropped and I had to start all over again. Fortunately the egg grader production went on during the war. For some reason or other the Government decided that eggs had to be sold by weight and this law was enforced more than ever before and we produced as many as eight per week for a long time.

"My main problem was to get people to work on the class of work which no one would argue was helpful to the war effort. This point of view became so prominent that in the end I had to take this production to Swineford and employ girls on it. How we got through with this inexperienced labour force is still a bit of a mystery. I can only put it down to the loyalty of my foreman, union and staff. One thing I am certain about is that all the packing stations that bought this machine didn't use them. Those who did use them suffered because of the poor labour we employed in building the machines.

"Meanwhile my drawing office and I worked like the devil to start up on new war work. I can honestly say that for three years I worked every day of the week 365 days a year to cope with the entirely new production. Many evenings I was busy in the factory until very late. We took on jobs for which our plant was very unsuitable; we took on three times as much as we could do.

"In fact I found as time went on that owing to hold ups in design material and one thing and another it paid to take on much more than we could possibly produce. Before the war broke out we had been producing the simplest of engineering units We were now making very complicated machines for the admiralty, machinery not only which required skilled men to assemble but the component parts had to be extremely accurate. In addition we made machine tools and thousands of special gun sights.

"By the end of the war we were employing about 850 people, we had expanded the production, spent thousands on plant and had become a fine engineering company. Truth was I had gained in experience tremendously both in machine design and the running of an engineering factory."

Although he had not actually succeeded in his bid to rejoin the military Harry was determined to wear a uniform during the Second World War and he achieved that by forming a Home Guard unit at Brecknells. As well as putting in the hours at the factory he took his turn fire-watching and went to meetings at Central Hall, Old Market, where fire-watching patrols were planned.

Brecknells Home Guard protected the factory and at one point got hold of an old tank and worked on it at the factory so they would be ready to see off a Nazi invasion.

He designed and built his own air raid shelter in the hallway in the family home. During one raid a bomb shell landed in the garden and buried itself six feet in the ground, but didn't explode.

The biggest fear was that the factories would become a target for the German bombers, especially now that intelligence might inform them that war work was being carried out there - after all Brecknells had been producing shells and munitions in the first war. It wasn't long before the fear was realised, as Harry wrote years later:

"The Germans made their first raid on Bristol and a fire incendiary fell on the works and whilst there was not extensive damage there was enough to make us realise that any day the whole place might be blown sky high and I should be left as poor as I was before I had taken on the responsibility of the company.

"I therefore thought out a scheme against this. It was not against the law to turn private companies into a public company. I contacted a financier in London and discussed this problem with him and discovered that it was possible to become a public company if the shares were taken over by a few friends. It didn't take long to find a few friends willing to buy some of the shares and in no time I had sold some of my shares for £4,000. This was indeed something for the future.

"My partners had agreed to the proposition and sold a number of shares equal to mine. Needless to say the financier got his rake off. It was after this had gone through I found myself the boss of the company and working harder than ever before. Many of the services staff were taken from us to help in other factories for the war effort. The best men in every department were taken and it was a most difficult problem trying to make unskilled labour do highly skilled jobs.

"I was told by other members of the management staff that I was attempting an impossible task but I succeeded. For instance I took a painter and trained him to operate a planing machine, I transferred clerks to calibrating tooling machines. I adopted a system of promotions and a higher wage packet and it worked wonders. Jobs, which highly skilled men had always been employed on, were given to women straight from houses to help with the war effort. Some had never had a job at all. Of course we weren't alone with this problem, most firms had to face up to the same sort of thing, but it required a lot of courage, drive and hard work and I couldn't afford to fail."

So, with a combination of clever management of the workforce, some financial trickery and a little invention - during the war years Harry designed many jigs and tools for improving and increasing production - Brecknells survived the war.

Harry knew that when the war ended the company's future was anything but assured, so he started planning for peacetime and in the immediate aftermath of war. As men were returning from fighting across Europe and beyond he set up systems and apprentice schemes that would mean the firm would also survive the tough days of post-war rationing. He said:

"So many firms fail because of their complacency. When you are busy and the money is rolling in that is the time to prepare for the future; that is the time to develop new ideas and to do the research which all new lines demand.

"Months before the war ended I decided that packing machinery was going to be one of the lines, food packing, because everyone must eat and the government was leaning toward greater hygiene. Furthermore the Germans had been leading the world in this industry. I would like to have gone much further in the packing industry, but we couldn't afford more draughtsmen, they were more valuable than diamonds. My chief designer gave up trying to recruit them so I then decided to tackle the problem from a long term angle.

"I picked up six of the best young boys in the works and put them in the drawing office. The chief nearly had a fit. He said: "I am already overwhelmed with work and to have to look after six young draughtsmen as well is beyond a joke".

"However I insisted and within six months these boys came through with flying colours all making first class designers. Needless to say I have continued with this policy ever since and the best boys go into the drawing office, which is the heart of any engineering business. Of course during their training period they were given a job a little beyond their ability, but that was conducive to quick training.

"Although chances were taken with design and production one must remember that we were about to enter a field with no experience whatsoever and there are many pitfalls in any new designs leave alone packing machines.

"My main problem of course was to change over from war production to some sort of peacetime production without losing any men and if possible making a reasonable profit at the end of the year. Of course a few Government contracts were allowed to drift on at a slow pace and fortunately some continued for a long time after the war and it was during this period when everyone had to really pull their weight. I took on anything offered me and often guessed the price in order to fill the factory. One job which I contracted to do might have broken us if I hadn't succeeded in getting a better price through re-negotiation.

"I spent thousands of pounds on new designs, new tools and development. I had no guarantee that it was going to be a success, just confidence in myself and my judgement of requirements. Within 18 months we were in production with a butter packer, printer, a modern egg grader and were already developing a new type of sugar packer which we hoped would swamp the field. Swamp the field it did and although we were up against the Americans, Germans and Swiss in no time this machine was redesigned and its speed increased from 50 per minute to 200. No doubt we had by now established ourselves as second to none in this type of work.

"Of course there were many many difficulties and sometimes mechanical problems arose for which there seemed no solution. But we stuck to it. I have spent dozens of sleepless nights on such problems.

"It was during such periods when I first realised how much we depend on each other; fitters would have nothing to do without designers. Designers would be no use without first class fitters, first class machinists and first class riveters, etc."

Harry also introduced incentive bonus schemes to keep the quality of production high. Throughout the war years the company was employing nearly 1,000 workers and Harry Dolman was the only director working with the company.

The vending machines, which had been the top sellers pre-war, could not re-commence production because of shortages of material and rationing. Harry's move into packaging proved successful with machines for packing sugar, flour, margarine and eggs, ensuring the future of the business.

The success of these machines - hastily invented at the end of the war - is shown by the fact that by 1958 the egg grading and packing machines won the gold medal at the Royal Dairy Show; in 1962 the firm won a gold medal at the same show for its latest high speed butter packing machine; in 1968 won a silver medal at the International Poultry Show for Auto Packing and egg grading machine with electric weighting and by 1968 was awarded the Queen's Award for Industry.

Before Brecknells began production of packing machines they had mostly been imported from Germany and Switzerland and eventually Brecknells took 90% of the home market and exported their machines worldwide.

The printer that Harry mentions, and an ice cream freezer, also proved successes for a short time after the war.

The firm also hit the headlines in the war when Queen Mary, wife of King George V, visited Bristol on January 13, 1942, and had a tour of the factory. For many years it was a mystery why the Royal Family should choose this particular factory to visit and why Harry

Dolman was the man pictured in the newspapers alongside the Queen showing her the production lines.

A huge crowd gathered for the visit and it helped to put the firm - and Harry Dolman - firmly into the minds of local people as a local success. The simple truth is that Harry heard that the Queen was staying at Badminton House to escape the bombing of London and he simply wrote a letter and sent it there. Within a week the visit took place.

But the workaholic attitude, spending hours and hours working rather than going home to his family, success as a businessman and mixing with people in high places, was taking its toll on Harry's private life.

His daughter Hazel remembers: "Dad was staying away from home more and more going on business trips. There was rationing of petrol and he said that was the reason he was staying in hotels and not coming home.

"He spent lots of time at Swineford in the old tumbledown building there that was converted into a fitting shop and foundry. He was always good to us and we saw the benefit of his success but it was clear that things were not so good between Mum and Dad.

"Then one day he moved into a room of his own. My mother divorced him but never made it absolute. From then on they lived separate lives in the same house.

"Mum cooked his breakfast and she would leave some supper for him. I suppose people would find it strange but it was just how things were with us. We just accepted it. I always got the impression that Mum was waiting for him to come back to her, but he never did.

"He was great with all his children. Frances was the first to get married in 1946. I got married in 1947 and he found a job within the firm for my husband Ray. He bought each of us a house when we married. He not only made good money from the business but he invested his money wisely."

The records show that Harry was named in a divorce case in December 1945. An ex-airman from Knowle was granted a decree nisi on the grounds of his wife's "misconduct" with Harry Dolman at a Brighton Hotel. Doris Dolman divorced her husband exactly seven months later because of his unacceptable behaviour.

ASHTON GATE

When Harry Dolman became a director of Bristol City Football Club in 1939 he could hardly have imagined that it was an association that would last for the rest of his life. The first season that he was on the board lasted just three games before it was suspended because of the Second World War.

As well as his efforts to ensure his business survived the war, he worked alongside his fellow board members to ensure that Bristol City survived as well. With no league matches, he helped to organise a few friendly games, some of which saw big players from other clubs turn out in Bristol City colours. Among them were Arthur Milton, of Arsenal, and Bill Shankly, of Preston North End, who later became the legendary manager of Liverpool.

The ground was bombed during the blitz on Bristol with the stand on the Winterstoke Road side of the pitch completely destroyed during one raid. Another time unexploded bombs penetrated into the terracing so that the ground had to be sealed off. The Covered End roof was damaged and with little income the club was in a sad state by the time a wartime cup competition was revived to keep interest going.

A few good footballers had found themselves working at BAC Bristol on war work and City were able to sign some of these and they had unearthed a new young star in Roy Bentley, a centre-forward destined to play at the highest level for England and Chelsea, who even as a teenager showed tremendous promise.

Just before football was about to resume in 1946, chairman George Jenkins took a strong Bristol City side on a tour of Denmark to prepare them for the season ahead. But money was so tight that he decided to sell the club's biggest asset. Bentley, despite the fact that he was a part-timer and had a full-time job at Avonmouth, was snapped up for a club record fee of £8,000. It meant the club had a little money - but it didn't please the fans who saw the season start without their star player.

City fan Tom Hopegood, who comes from a long line of City supporters from the St Philip's Marsh area of Bristol, said: "There had been so much poverty in Bristol before the war and the City matches were one way to escape. For example George's Brewery held its annual staff outing to a City away game as a special treat for the workers.

"Harry Dolman was the whizz-kid of the day. Everyone was very pleased that he was at the club, as he looked capable of taking it to a different level. George Jenkins had a few bob, but he was a fish-and-chip shop owner from Redcliffe Hill. Harry Dolman was an inventor, an ideas man, someone who was trading across the world. It seems obvious now that he would be more ambitious and have more ideas than the board that was in place.

"Harry thought like the fans. He didn't like it when Roy Bentley was transferred and he watched carefully as the board negotiated compensation for the damage done to the stand. I think he finally made his voice known when Cyril Williams, who was also loved by the fans and a fantastic player, was also sold. He went to West Bromwich Albion for £500 and Cliff Edwards in return."

Harry told of those immediate post-war years:

"Little did I know then that Bristol City would cost tens of thousands before I finished with the club. In my opinion Mr George Jenkins, the chairman at that time, was a little man with a great deal of energy. A little ruthless, perhaps, fair, but always the boss.

"If anyone on the board objected to any suggestions of his they

were asked if they wanted to be chairman, in other words he told us what we had to do and no messing. Unfortunately the war came after we had played one match and the league programme was cancelled. Clubs who wished to do so were allowed to play friendlies and later on a local league programme was arranged. George and Bob Hewison did all the work, picking a team from guest players who happened to be stationed nearby in the forces on whatever they were doing.

"I attended matches home and away when I could, but I had now become Managing Director of Brecknell, Munro & Rogers, the company I had been with since 1921. I was the only director on the spot working at the factory employing nearly a thousand people, so I had my hands full, but I attended every (Bristol City) board meeting and gained a lot of experience and kept helping out with club bills.

"Very little of interest happened during the war from a football point of view except that the premises were badly bombed, completely destroying the west stand. The pitch was hit by bombs as was the terracing. The Covered End was also in a very sorry state.

"We, of course, received certain sums of money for war damage, but it was badly negotiated and was not nearly enough to do the repairs necessary. These things were all left to the chairman.

"Fortunately, the manager Bob Hewison had been busy and had signed some young boys – to quote two - Roy Bentley and Cyril Williams. Both, however, were sold; Roy Bentley, before he played a league match for Bristol City and Cyril Williams after one season, because of the heavy debts of the club and the bank were very loathe to allow an overdraft.

"Cyril Williams was not sold, as has been said by some people, because he wanted 10/- a week more. We had to find money to pay debts and by this time I was able to understand the feeling between the supporters and the board.

"I was also present at the meeting when the chairman and manager received a vote of no confidence. Up to then, annual meetings were attended by not more than a dozen people. At this meeting there were 70 people or so present. However, the vote of no confidence was proposed, seconded and carried with an overwhelming majority. George Jenkins did an extraordinary thing – he stayed in the chair for the remainder of the evening.

"Several days went by before the new chairman was elected. I had no intention of taking it on, or even allowing my name to go forward. I did not even know what the procedure should be in such matters.

"However, much to my great surprise, they begged me to take it. The only opposition being from Arthur Sperring. He badly wanted it and eventually agreed to my having it for one year and it was understood he would then take over. Unfortunately, Arthur died before the next season started and when the election of the chairman came up the following year, I was unanimously asked to continue. I promised in a general way that we would not sell any player who was an asset to the club unless the circumstances were out of our control. I kept this promise."

Those meetings were in 1949. On March 8 the manager Bob Hewison had resigned after a row with the board over team selection, even though he had been given a new contract just three months earlier.

The vote of no confidence took place at the Annual General Meeting in the Grand Hotel, Bristol, and at a subsequent meeting Harry agreed to become chairman for a year. So began Harry Dolman's 25 year stint as Chairman of Bristol City Football Club. During that time he had one main stated aim: to get the club up into the top flight - the First Division - where they might play the likes of Arsenal, Bolton and Chelsea. But he took over a club still suffering from wartime damage, with a fan base angry that two of the best players had been sold and languishing in the lower reaches of the football league.

He told how he went about changing things, starting with the new stand that had been built on the Winterstoke Road side of the ground, housing dressing rooms and the seats for the board of directors:

"I was scared stiff. The bills came in faster and more frequently than ever and what is more, the football management gave instructions that old transfer fees had to be settled. The bank did not seem very keen to help in any way so I began to formulate schemes to get in some extra cash. I introduced a scheme of advertising.

"I sold the programme for a couple of years and the garage which had been built during the war, I purchased for a couple of thousand and re-sold it at £600 a year for five years, paid in advance. I sold the garage at the end of five years for about £6,000 with a retainer clause. This produced another £4,000 some years later. We sold a few season tickets for five years, paid.

"The pitch had been bombed. The main stand was destroyed and we were left with a small wooden stand which was unsafe and condemned. It had a capacity of less than 1,000.

"Before I became chairman a licence to build a new stand had been applied for. We were to be compensated by the War Damage Commission, but the amount we received was not nearly enough to cover the cost of the new stand. Material and labour was short and the stand put forward was inadequate and I think very badly designed.

"The result was a lot of complaints about leg room for our spectators, so much so that something had to be done about it and as I was now chairman of the board, I took the job in hand to alter the seating and, as we had no money, I did it at my own expense. A few of my own work people helped out and we increased the leg room in each row by 2". We were years paying off the money for this stand.

"I am not proud of this stand. It was all done in too much of a hurry. In those days, the chairman would ask individual directors to carry out certain tasks and no-one else would know anything about it.

"Another club within 100 miles of Bristol received twice as much as we did for war damage. They built a larger and better stand. Someday I hope, when we have a lot of money, our old stand will be demolished and something much better built. That is the best side of the pitch for spectators and the stand should hold 6,000 to 7,000 people."

Note: Harry wrote these words over 40 years before the redevelopment of the stand which saw the giant South Stand built that now dominates the skyline at Ashton Gate.

"The Covered End was in such a shocking state that we were instructed to do something about it at once or cease to use it. On top of which we were still in the 3rd Division. People said then the same as I've been hearing since – "Don't spend money on the ground, spend it on building the team".

"The pitch was now in such a shocking state that something had to be done. But houses had to be found for every player signed on because of the housing shortage.

"I was inundated with letters about the bad pitch, the leaking stand and Covered End and bad terracing. People complained they had not been able to see when we were blessed with large attendances. So we decided to tackle the pitch first. Remember we had no money, but somehow or other we found £20,000 to spend on the pitch in the next three or four years. In fact, the pitch was completely relaid, raised 20 inches and the drains relaid, but a lot of work had to be done and, of course, paid for. After this we built up the terracing and re-sited the turnstiles, costing pretty near another £10,000 when new toilets were included.

"We then set about the Covered End. It had to be painted, built up at the rear to make it safe. The roof was treated to make it watertight. "This must have cost another £20,000."

The War Damage Commission had agreed to give Bristol City £16,500 for the rebuilding work and in compensation for the damage caused by the German raids in January and April 1941. The figure had been based on a valuation in 1939 of the stand being worth £7,500 plus 120 per cent. But by the 1950s, when the work was actually being carried out, there was a steel shortage and some of the money that Harry Dolman found came from the newly-formed supporters club.

He struck a deal with the supporters that they would be given a room in the new stand to meet in if they could raise money for steel. Some £3,000 was handed over and the 51 Club formed in 1951 as an executive supporters club. The stand was finally open fully in 1953.

But Harry Dolman was still determined to improve facilities at Ashton Gate and he turned his mind to floodlighting. The league did not allow games to be played under light but those teams and stadiums that had floodlighting were attracting big crowds for the novelty of evening games that seemed to generate their own special atmosphere under the new lighting.

Of course as an inventor Harry realised that the cheapest and easiest way to get lighting installed at Ashton Gate was for him to invent them himself - and that is exactly what he did. He told the story:

"Soon after I became chairman of the board, the question of installing floodlighting and other ground changes was frequently being raised.

"I remember how my fellow director Percy Bennet was determined to increase the capacity of the ground from 40,000 to 80,000. The only way to do this, he said, was to turn the pitch around 90 degrees so that the goal posts would have been in front of the stands. I kept asking the question: "Why make the capacity greater when we don't fill the ground now?" He insisted that in time we would be getting 100,000 gates. He also pressed for the introduction of floodlighting which induced me to put this in when I did.

"As usual there was no money, so I volunteered to put in the floodlights myself. At that time no-one knew quite what was going to happen. It was an experiment. Even today I believe the best way to light up a football pitch is from above and not from the sides or corners. It should also be easier to clean the lamps.

"There are not many people willing to climb up the towers to carry out this work. I would like to see a tower for each quarter of the pitch and an arm extended from each tower exactly similar to the jib on a building site which raised and lowered the building material. Two great features about this method of lighting would be (1) no glare to spectators and (2) the arm carrying the light could be lowered for cleaning.

"However, I offered to install lighting and knowing so little about it, I designed the simplest method known to me and told the club to pay me when they could. As it happened, we did extraordinarily well with our first installation. I am not pretending it was wonderful, but the fact remains we played about six friendly matches, three rugby matches on the ground and the extra income was at least £25,000. The lights cost me £5,000 and the club only paid me £3,500, which was the estimated amount I thought it would cost. However, this proved that floodlighting was a success and had come to stay, so 10 years later we installed something better costing nearly £30,000. Again I would remind you we had no money."

Harry's floodlights saw seven 40 foot high metal pylons installed on each side of the pitch, each with three lamps on the top. They stood in front of spectators but as most people were standing they could simply shift a few feet to get a view. Soon six more pylons were put up - three at each end of the pitch.

Big crowds were attracted to the friendly matches played under the lights with Arsenal, Spurs and East Fife among the opposition and top European teams also brought to Bristol to provide the entertainment. It wasn't until February 1957 that the first league game was played under floodlights - still under Harry Dolman's design. City duly won that game 3-0 against Notts County.

But those early days as chairman were not just about improving facilities at Ashton Gate. With Bob Hewison resigning just weeks before Dolman took over, his first task was to try to find a manager for the team.

Several top managers were in the frame, including Bill Dodgin at Southampton; but Harry really wanted the Irish International Peter Docherty to join as a player-manager. He was doing great things at international level and as an inside forward with Huddersfield Town. Harry believed he might be the young manager to take Bristol City to the top flight but he failed in his bid. Instead Charlton Athletic Assistant Manager Bob Wright moved to Bristol City and became the first of just five managers to be in charge of the club in the 25 years that Harry Dolman served as chairman.

But Wright only lasted in the post for 14 months, quitting at the end of the 1949-1950 season and telling the media at the time that he had not been given the free hand that he had been promised, a clear reference to the fact that Harry Dolman was maybe a little too "hands on" with his chairmanship. He was learning fast that being the boss at Brecknells was not the same as being the boss at a football club.

MANAGERS, MEN AND MANAGEMENT

B y the time Harry Dolman became chairman of Bristol City he had decades of experience of business under his belt and a clear view of how it should be conducted. Brecknell, Munro & Rogers he ran as a kind of benevolent dictatorship. He had enormous respect from the people he worked with. They knew it was his inventions that had at least started the business off and the motto among many staff was "don't mess with Harry".

Derek Andrews worked at Brecknells from 1957 to 1968, firstly as an apprentice and then later in the drawing office, making lifelong friends in the process.

He said: "Harry Dolman was the gaffer. The days when Harry were in charge were fantastic. It was real engineering where people tried to solve problems and worked together. Things were often worked out on the back of a cigarette packet and then tried out.

"Engineering hadn't really changed since the days before the war and computerisation hadn't come along so it was a time when people were at the heart of success. I worked on the egg grading and packing machines while others worked on the butter packing and fruit machines.

"I became a member of the drawing office when I was 20 and Harry's office was across the yard and the experimental work was all done in another office, which was through a hatch. Harry was always interested in the experimental and new work and a man called Wally Knee was our usual link to him.

"But three or four times a month Harry Dolman would come into our section We were all very young and would be quite excited if he spoke to us. He had his chauffeur, Bob, who would drive his

Rolls Royce and it was exciting to us as young men and all keen on sport that he was involved in Bristol City and in other sports.

"We always called him "Mr" Dolman and he was feared when he came in as we knew how powerful and important he was. There was a great deal of respect, but that was the way that bosses were treated in those days by younger people.

"Although the machinery we used was basic, fantastic progress was made. We got the egg grading machines up to weighing 12,800 eggs an hour, weighing, grading and packing them using the principles that Harry had invented in the 1920s. It wasn't until the mid-1960s that the business started looking at introducing electronics.

"We all worked together and we would all socialise and go out and drink together and the company had a lively social scene. We would all go to The Webbington, south of Bristol, and there was a lot of drinking and fun had. The management joined in and Harry would appear in fancy dress and have as many drinks as everyone else.

"At the Christmas socials he would dress up as Father Christmas and hand out presents to the children of employees. Everyone in the drawing office would save up to pay for the Christmas night out and Harry was always invited and paid for his own meal and drinks. At those events he joined in just as one of the lads."

Harry had developed a firm philosophy about how to manage people - one that he was following at Brecknells and which he attempted to introduce into the world of football, where he believed it would work just as well, but where he didn't quite ever have the control he had over his own business.

Harry wrote down how he liked to incentivise staff at Brecknells and his management theory. It tells how his views were shaped by his own experience and how he came to improve pay for those working for him at the company. It is reproduced here:

Men and Management.

I place Men before Management, because without the Men there can be no Management.

On becoming part of the Management in about 1930 I had some advantage in the fact that I had been managed. I had been one of the men. I knew what it was like to be short of money, clothes and sometimes food, not forgetting the many other things that are essential to the happiness of the ordinary man. Once I joined the Management, therefore, I made up my mind that these things would be altered for the people who worked with me.

The first essential is that employees should have a good living wage with, as far as possible, prospects of improving their standards of living by hard work. I am not a believer in incentives for individuals but I do believe in incentives for all. For example, in my opinion, it is wrong to pay a commission to a salesmen and yet give nothing to the man who designs, processes, progresses or makes the article you sell. Every man, whatever his position or job, is a part of the machine, and all deserve equal encouragement.

When I became a Director of the Company there existed in the works an Incentive Bonus Scheme, the system being that a certain time was allowed for each job: for say turning, drilling, fitting etc, and if the man did the job in less time than was allowed he was given a bonus. If, however, he took longer than was allowed, then the extra time went against the time he had gained. The main thing wrong with this system was that only those people working on jobs which could be timed could participate. Storemen, viewers, inspectors, drawing office staff, clerks and many other could not be included.

There was also the problem of the fast and slow worker. A worker may be slow, but otherwise he may be extraordinarily good. Then there was the case of the man who looks at the time allowed and will not attempt to get down to the job due to the fact that he has already made up his mind that the time allowed is insufficient.

As can be seen, therefore, this bonus system was full of moans and fiddles. Many other modified schemes were tried and all had similar faults.

I had read about the Liberal Policy. I had also read the policies of the other political parties, and in spite of the fact that my parents were very strong Conservatives, I decided that the Liberals had the best policy and I came to the conclusion that everyone was entitled to a share in the profits.

I introduced the Profit Sharing Scheme, almost immediately after World War II, and I made up my mind that if the profits of the Company increased and the shareholders were given higher dividends then the employees of the Company would have a correspondingly higher share, and in assessing this at the appropriate time I, if anything, leaned on the side of the work people.

The first year this came into force, all employees were paid a bonus of seven-and-a-half per cent. Within ten years this had risen to 20% of their weekly or monthly pay packet and it was manifestly clear that the Company could pay better wages and so we decided to consolidate some of the bonus into the weekly or monthly pay packet.

Of course the manager of a football club has a very special role to fulfil. He is the person who gets all the plaudits and praise when things go well and he is the first to lose his job when things go badly. In the modern game the relationship between the often billionaire owners and the managers is fascinating, especially when the owner comes from a different culture and has bought into the English game.

The dynamic between the owner and the manager of a football

club is always a tough one, the owner investing hard-earned cash into the club for the manager to spend in the hope that it brings success, and both having to suffer the anger of the fans when it doesn't.

Rarely do football club chairmen have the opportunity to talk candidly about their relationship with managers and Harry Dolman's pre-season messages through his 25 years pretty well all followed the pattern of saying that Bristol City at last had a good team in place with a mixture of good young players and experience; that the manager seemed the right man for the job to secure promotion and that the fans could look forward to some improvements in the facilities at Ashton Gate.

Amongst his papers, however, is a hand-written page entitled "what I expect of managers of football clubs", which sets out in no uncertain terms the skills he, as chairman, expected and looked for when he was appointing a manager. It makes fascinating reading:

What I expect of managers of football clubs:
To be in complete control and understand what is required to be successful. In my time with Bristol City we did NOT have one in this category.

A manager must know football. He must have the will and determination to WIN and be able to instil this into the team he is managing.

He must set a good example before, during and after the matches.

He must be able to manage all players, the old as well as the young boys.

He must be loyal to his players, his club and everyone assisting him.

When a player has to be bought, he should know exactly what is wanted. A player who is not going to fit in is dear at any price and the money is wasted. I would never, ever buy a First Division throw out with a bad reputation. I would always look in the Third or Fourth Division for the best and most skilful players there. They are cheaper, more loyal and usually better value. Good managers in the First Division seem to be able to unload their unwanted players to clubs in a desperate state.

A good manager should know of a player for every position in his side – players who are, or may be, available. When teams are doing well, managers become complacent, but in fact that is the time to make sure success continues. Most managers sign a lot of players they hope will make it. They can't decide which will be useful and thousands of pounds are wasted in wages.

In the early days of my chairmanship I had quite a lot to do with signing players. I do not mean I selected them or judged their ability. Most players, even young schoolboys as well as old professionals, wanted something under the counter, or they wanted a job at the end of their playing days – or to be put in a job if they did not make the grade. They made all sorts of demands. This has all stopped since the players were made free to make their own contracts, but I gave young boys a job - sometimes gave their father a job. I also gave jobs to old professionals at the end of their playing days.

Altogether it involved me in a good deal of cash payment and other responsibilities. It was that or not being able to sign the player we wanted.

Harry's missive on what he expected from a manager was written later in life and maybe with the hindsight of experience. In the summer of 1950 he was looking for a replacement for Bob Wright and aware that the team also needed experienced player. The idea of tempting an older, experienced player who might turn his hand to management still appealed.

He had not been able to sign Peter Docherty as a player manager and had watched enviously as he had instead become player manager at Doncaster and was now combining that with the manager's job for Northern Ireland where he was introducing revolutionary training tactics.

Docherty was still out of reach, but Dolman and his fellow directors had no less than 12 applicants to choose from for the vacant job. Some of them had impressive CVs and backgrounds. But Harry Dolman had the idea of a player manager and he persuaded the directors that Pat Beasley, a 38-year-old player from Fulham looking to move into management, was the man to take Bristol City forward. The deal was sealed with a five year contract, the longest the club had ever given at that time, as Harry Dolman wanted to see some consistency to build for the long term. A five year contract also meant that Beasley could play for the next two years and then concentrate on management alone after that.

Although the club had been without a manager Harry had been making moves to strengthen the team and Beasley was to find himself playing alongside a familiar face - his former Fulham team-mate Syd Thomas. It had been while doing the deal to bring Thomas to Ashton Gate that Harry had become familiar with Beasley. He told how that signing was made in his own words, an account which is in stark contrast to the lives of big-money footballers today:

"During the period when we were managerless, I had been in touch with Bill Dodgin, who was manager of Fulham, about Syd Thomas. £10,000 had been offered and it was now for Syd to agree. It was close season and Bill said he was home in Aberystwyth.

"Off I went with fellow director George Jones in my car, arriving quite late in the afternoon. When we got there, almost the first person we saw was a young man delivering bread. He had an old-fashioned bread van and I had been told that Syd's family was in the baking business. I was tempted to ask him if he knew where I could find Syd Thomas.

"However, I proceeded to the address I had been given and met his sister and a relation. She immediately said he was out delivering bread, but would soon be home. Sure enough, it was Syd Thomas whom we had seen earlier.

"Syd came to Bristol next day with me and signed for us. George Jones and I had great difficulty in finding a place to stay in Aberystwyth and eventually booked in at a place, but we could have no food and the room had one bed but no other furniture. George and I laughed until our sides ached. Syd was a brilliant winger, but only played in six or seven matches, after which he had to give up football for medical reasons. We tried to get back some of the fee paid, but Fulham would not agree."

Harry's memory is not quite accurate as the records show that Syd Thomas played a total of 13 games for City before he was taken seriously ill with tuberculosis and was not able to play again. Harry attempted to get compensation from Fulham in the form of a reserve player for free and although the Football League was called in they refused to make any ruling and Harry's efforts to sign undoubtedly a top player proved to be an expensive mistake.

At a Bristol Round Table Luncheon in November 1950, at the Berkeley Cafe, Harry Dolman gave vent to some of the frustrations he felt as chairman of Bristol City talking about the challenge ahead, the attitude of the Bristol public and the rules of the game.

He told the audience of local business people:

"I think there is no city in England that is so badly served for football as Bristol. It is not due to bad management or direction, but because

Bristol people are only lukewarm to football.

"In a city of the size of Bristol you should be getting gates of 40,000 every Saturday. If we were doing that we could spend more money on players and have a better chance of getting a team together without worrying about the risk. What a wonderful thing it would be if we had a team in the First Division and going to the Cup Final?

"If we could get to the First Division we would have our share of international matches here and we should get thousands of people flocking into the city bringing their womenfolk and spending money in the hotels, restaurants and shops.

"We want Bristol people to take an interest in Bristol football teams and I am sure they would find they would get some benefit from it."

He also took the occasion to back calls for substitutes to be introduced to the game so that teams did not have to battle on with 10 men after a player was injured, saying that allowing a substitute to come on as a replacement would also speed the latter half of games up and make it more exciting for spectators.

The comments about Bristolians being "lukewarm" did not go unchallenged with supporters writing to the Western Daily Press to say that City's average attendance was better than anyone in the Third Division North and third in the Southern section.

One person, who said he had supported the club for 40 years, hit back in a reader's letter saying: "It is high time that your readers contested Mr Dolman's allegations. He and his colleagues alone are responsible for the club's affairs. If they will remain in the slap-happy section of the league they cannot expect first league support. The management are in the same position as that of a shop-keeper. Unless they stock the class of goods required by the public, customers will be few and far between, Moreover they will stay away. And this is what has happened at Ashton Gate.

"When will the directors of the club wake up to the fact that sportsmen are sick to death of third rate football and all its implications. Mr Dolman and his colleagues have inherited the "third-rate football complex legacy" left them by former directors. And the chairman of the club will, I have no doubt, admit that not so long ago his club was sitting pretty and well on the way out of the Third Division. The then directors sold the very players capable of winning promotion. Were the directors lukewarm? Or the clubs supporters?"

Such exchanges showed Harry Dolman that it was a very different business trying to run a football club where passions ran higher than his day to day business.

Over at Brecknell, Munro & Rogers the money was rolling in at this time and Harry Dolman was able to balance perfectly his work at the football club with continuing to expand the management team and products being produced in his firm.

It was international markets that were proving the big success as this extract from trade magazine The Machinery Market, from the early 1950s, indicates:

"Mr Harry Dolman, chairman and managing director of Brecknell, Munro and Rogers Ltd, Pennywell Road, Bristol, is sailing to America shortly to seek fresh markets for some of the firm's products, and to appoint an agent to look after their interests. He will be taking with him patterns of new machines. The butter and sugar packeting machines, which sell well in this country and overseas, can wrap packs at the rate of 120 a minute. A limited number of the butter packing machines have already been distributed in the United States but now it is hoped to enter this market in "a really big way". Mr Dolman's tour is expected to last about a month."

When he returned the Bristol Evening Post reported: "Since

he has been back in Bristol following his business trip to North America, Mr Harry J Dolman managing director of Brecknell Munro and Rogers, has been almost consistently in conference.

"Very substantial orders have resulted from his visit. Like many other industrialists, Mr Dolman has found great value in personal contacts with the keen businessmen of the American continent. The trade stemming from that trip is, I hear, of the type that will recur annually. All of it, of course, will earn vital dollars."

Certainly his involvement with Bristol City was not going to result in Harry "taking his eye off the ball" in his own engineering business. It was going from strength to strength and his faith in the workforce and his fellow managers enabled it to continue growing. His method of travelling to do business face-to-face had paid off with Brecknells and he was sure he could transfer that same ability to help Bristol City get out of the Third Division and start climbing towards his dream of them being a top flight side.

He knew the key was finding the best players who had the club at their heart and who would fit in with his new young manager. Harry set off on his travels again, but this time it was not to the USA or in to the depths of Wales - he sought out a player in his old familiar home area of Wiltshire.

ATYEO AND PROMOTION

People entering Bristol City's Ashton Gate stadium from Winterstoke Road are confronted by a life-sized bronze statue of arguably the team's greatest ever player, John Atyeo. Certainly he was a prolific goal-scorer, putting the ball in the net 351 times during 645 appearances for the team, between 1951 and 1966 when he retired from the game.

Sculpted by Tom Murphy, it shows Atyeo, arms aloft, celebrating a goal - or three - against arch-rivals Bristol Rovers. At the other end of the ground, now used by away supporters, is the Atyeo Stand, named in honour of this true legend of south Bristol football.

The reason that John Atyeo signed for Bristol City and stayed there so long as a player, despite many attempts to lure him away by so-called bigger clubs, was down to one man - Harry Dolman. Harry Dolman's daughter, Hazel, remembers taking a telephone call at home from a football contact of her father's one day when he was out.

She said: "The man asked me to take a note and to ask my dad to ring him back. He said he wanted to talk to him about signing John Atyeo. I remember writing the name on a piece of paper and passing it on to dad when he came in. John Atyeo lived in Wiltshire and that was the area dad came from so he was immediately interested in him."

Harry Dolman himself revealed in notes that he went to see Walter Atyeo, John's father, six times at his home in Dilton Marsh before he was able to persuade him to let his son join Bristol City. Other teams were interested and on one of those six occasions Harry saw a car belonging to Bristol Rovers manager Bert Tann parked nearby.

Portsmouth were the best team in the country at the time.

Bolstered by good footballers who had served in the Royal Marines and the Royal Navy during the war, they won back-to-back league titles in 1948/59 and 1950/51.

They had spotted the talents of John Atyeo, who had been making a big name for himself at non-league Westbury United, in Wiltshire, and even though he was only a teenager and playing amateur football they put him in their team in November 1950 at Fratton Park against Charlton Athletic and against Arsenal at home in March. Both games ended in draws.

The strapping six-foot teenager, already a youth international, didn't score but to make two appearances in the top flight for the league champions was a massive achievement. His family, however, wanted him to keep his feet on the ground, gain some qualifications so that he had something to fall back on outside football and were resisting the overtures of Portsmouth to sign him permanently and add him to their top-notch squad.

Harry Dolman was not likely to bow to the league champions. Even though his team were only in the third tier he set about persuading Walter Atyeo that his boy's best prospects lay with Bristol City.

Many football historians over the years have said that at the time the likes of Reading, QPR, Arsenal, Spurs and Swindon were also talking to John Atyeo's father wanting the signature.

But none had the experienced business brain of Harry Dolman and his wheeling and dealing and determination to succeed meant that he was always likely to be the one who got the deal over the line - he wouldn't take no for an answer and negotiated and drew up a personal contract with Atyeo's father that not only ensured he joined Bristol City but the clauses within it were a major part in keeping him on board for so many years.

They included a clause guaranteeing that John Atyeo would

always be the best paid player on the team's books; a clause saying he should be allowed to stay at home and finish his apprenticeship as a quantity surveyor; a clause saying he should be allowed to drive a car to Bristol for training and clauses giving a donation of £100 and a fund-raising friendly game against Bristol City for his amateur club Westbury United.

Another clause saying that he could never be transferred without his father's consent was vetoed by the football authorities but by then Harry Dolman was trusted by Walter Atyeo and a handshake on that matter sufficed.

Atyeo, who conducted himself impeccably both on and off the field - he was never booked - received a £10 signing on fee and started on £12 a week.

Having secured one of the best young prospects in English football Harry set about boosting the team further in a bid to get the team promoted and provide manager Beasley with the skills he needed. Top of his list was the experienced Cyril Williams, who he had been sorry to see go to West Bromwich Albion.

Harry said of him:

> "I was responsible for bringing Cyril Williams back to Bristol City. In my opinion, he was one of our most brilliant forwards and could lay on the passes which produced goals. We never expected to lose any match and always talked about how many goals we might score."

West Bromwich Albion wanted £6,000 for Williams but Harry Dolman moved into his best negotiating mode and secured his services for £4,500. The season started with high hopes but ended with Bristol City 15th in the table. The drive for promotion within Harry Dolman could not be stopped.

With extra money coming in from the floodlit friendly games

and a new supporters club - called the 51 Club after the year it was founded - helping to pay for the new stand and providing a source of support and funding, the focus for Harry Dolman was winning promotion as soon as possible. In the 1952-53 season the club finished in fifth place - just five points behind the league leaders who were taking the leap up to the division above - Bristol Rovers.

Said Harry Dolman:

> "Instead of promotion for Bristol City it was promotion for Bristol Rovers. To me this was a blow. I never thought the Rovers could rise to this, but they fully deserved it and it was a great side that gained this reward for them. Had they concentrated on the youngsters around Bristol I believe they would have gone on to the 1st Division but somehow Bristol City seemed to sign most of the local boys. The Rovers promotion, however, only spurred us on."

With the near-neighbours from Eastville now lording it in the division above Harry redoubled his efforts, continuing to back his manager as they climbed to third place the following year. The dream was finally achieved in the 1954-55 season and to make sure that the club got over the line he acted in bringing in England and Arsenal star Arthur Milton in February 1955. Milton had already announced that he planned to retire from football at the end of that season.

Harry Dolman remembers:

> "Another dash I made was to Arsenal for Arthur Milton. Pat Beasley was manager at Bristol City and accompanied me. Arthur did not want to continue playing football and would not be persuaded otherwise. I talked with Tom Whittaker, the Arsenal manager, and we agreed a fee of £4,000 – the cheapest transfer ever if we could have persuaded Arthur Milton to continue playing.

"Tom agreed to repay half the fee if Arthur ceased playing at the end of that season. No-one knew a word about it until he was actually signed about midday on a Monday. I persuaded him to join Bristol City, although he made it clear that he was packing the game in at the end of that season."

Having signed a star player you might think that all Harry had to do was sit back in the Director's Box with a fat cigar and enjoy watching his team win the league. But football is not like that. Years later Harry Dolman was asked to recount the most exciting match he had ever seen at Bristol City - he found it impossible to choose, but his account of the end of that first promotion season, which he scribbled down in pencil in answer to the question, shows that he suffered all the anxiety and excitement of every football fan.

He wrote:

"I have been asked to write an article about the most exciting match. There have been so many since I became connected with Bristol City, I would not know which to select, so I have chosen to write about the last days when we won promotion for the first time during my chairmanship.

"The worry, the anxiety, the thrills and the days of waiting I shall never forget. We had to play three matches. We were at the top and points in front with Leyton Orient breathing down our necks in second place. They could catch up with us if we lost and they won. I used to travel with the team a lot then and I've never known such a confident lot of players as our boys were. They never talked of losing. They knew they were going to win. It was only a question of how many goals we should win by.

"It was a long time between one Saturday and the next, waiting for the 2 points which would make us secure. Sometimes in bed I would lay awake thinking about it, so although I felt reasonably confident I used to think sometimes – suppose we lost all three of our remaining matches? It was terrible.

"I remember I had attended a snooker competition at my club. The next round was the last eight and I was drawn against a person I could beat easily. We had a job to find a suitable date for this match and to get it settled we agreed to play on a Saturday morning. Bristol City had to play Newport in the afternoon – one of our last three matches. During the snooker game I just could not concentrate. My thoughts were at Ashton Gate. I had been reading every bit of news about the County – how they were going to stop our gallop into the Second Division. Of course, I lost the snooker match. Newport seemed to be a thorn in our side.

"I remember another season when they beat us twice. They were on the bottom and we were near the top. The four points they took from us that year, I believe, stopped us from going up.

"However, coming back to the point, we drew with Newport and the Orient only drew and we were virtually safe and did we celebrate! I never saw so much champagne. A friend of mine gave me a huge cake with a football pitch marked out on it.

"Pat Beasley was our player/manager and what an example he set to the rest of the team. He just worked and worked. I admired him more than any player wearing our colours. Jack White was another player I had a great admiration for, but it is unfair of me to pick out individuals because the whole team was great.

"Arthur Milton helped considerably, winning the last but one match of the season against Bournemouth almost entirely on his own. We were outplayed until about 10 minutes from the end when Milton ran with the ball from a position well in our opponent's half and finished with a brilliant shot, which beat the goalie. Result 1-0 in our favour."

The consistent scoring of Atyeo, the passes of Cyril Williams and the top class international talent of Arthur Milton, brought in on a gamble and an unorthodox promise by Harry Dolman, and had got Bristol City into the second tier of English football. There was no doubt that the chairman's business acumen, willingness to talk to people face-to-face, and sheer determination to get his own way had played a major part in achieving the success. It was time to celebrate.

Harry Dolman's grandson, Tony Dolman, inherited two LP-sized metallic disks – recorded by Bristol & West Recording Service of 6 Park Row, Bristol. They had been kept carefully by Harry for many years, so were obviously quite precious. The story Tony was told was that they contained audio recordings of a Brecknell, Dolman and Rogers board meeting and that Harry could be heard on there giving a speech. As part of the research for this book a machine was found that could decipher the disk. When the disk was played it started with the cheery sound of Al Jolson singing "Red Red Robin" - always a popular song of celebration in the years before Adge Cutler wrote "Drink Up Thy Zider" - and the rest is a news report of the celebrations following that first promotion under Harry Dolman's chairmanship.

Bristol's Lord Mayor is heard addressing the cheering crowd at Ashton Gate, when the trophy is presented, with the words: "Mr Dolman, ladies and gentlemen, this is a great occasion. I congratulate Bristol City on a well-earned promotion. They won promotion by a good margin but next year we want to see them win promotion to the first division."

To huge cheers from the thousands gathered at Ashton Gate Harry Dolman took the microphone and said: "This, ladies and gentlemen, is the happiest day of my life. Last week when I heard we won promotion I nearly cried with joy".

The team are heard singing in the bath. They had won promotion in the end by a clear nine points over their nearest rivals Leyton Orient; winning more games than any other side in all four divisions - 10 more than Chelsea who that year won the first division title.

They had started the season with a 13 match unbeaten run, had a wobble in December and January and ended the season with an 18 match unbeaten run. They scored 101 goals and conceded 47 - only Blackburn scored more goals that season but they had a worse goal average.

All the facts are laid out on the disks that Harry kept along with interviews with the captain Jack White, manager Pat Beasley, young goal-scoring sensation John Atyeo, Arthur Milton and Harry Dolman himself.

Pat Beasley is every inch the typical manager, saying: "I said when I came give me five years and we'll try to do something. Now our ambition is realised and everyone is very proud. We have had a marvellous team spirit here and have done this not as one man but as a team."

Jack White said: "After two years of near things we have achieved this through teamwork and all pulling together and fighting for each other. From what I have seen at Bristol Rovers I don't think we have got much to worry about next season."

Atyeo admitted that, like Harry Dolman, the run in to the championship had taken its toll. He told reporters: "I got into such a state I couldn't sleep or eat hardly anything. It came out all right in the end."

Harry Dolman praised his fellow board members for backing the club. He said:

"They are mostly businessmen but I believe we are the only club in the country with a parson on the board. One of them would make a good broadcasting commentator. He talks about the match from beginning to end. Never heard anyone better than he is at describing the game.

"I suppose there is a limit to everything but the board has been pretty good at backing the team. They have done it for five years. We are anything but rich but we are potentially wealthy. As chairman of the club it is my duty to see they get it back and as quickly as possible. This promotion is going to make a lot of difference to us.

"I believe the gates next year will be 25,000 average. We have lived very comfortably on 16,000 to 17,000 gates but if we can get 25,000 gates that will be at least another £800 a week gross, which is rather a lot of money.

"I would say that on promotion the club has spent £40,000 on the ground for the stand and putting it in condition and about the same amount on players - but have got quite a bit back that we spent on players."

Asked if he regarded chairmanship of the football club as "business" Harry tells the reporter: "No, it is good fun. Football is a business and from my point of view it is just fun… and I just love it."

In May 1955 everything seemed to be just right for Harry Dolman, who was at the peak of his powers. He was a success in business, driving his Rolls Royce around and puffing on his Churchill-style cigars; the innovations kept rolling out of Brecknells and at his football club he was being cheered to the rafters as the man who had financed and masterminded Bristol City reaching the second Division, where next year they would meet the likes of Sheffield Wednesday, Leeds, Liverpool, Blackburn, Leicester, Nottingham Forest, West Ham…and, of course, their old rivals, Bristol Rovers.

THE MAN WITH
THE MIDAS TOUCH

T hroughout the 1950s and into the 1960s, as Harry Dolman settled in to football chairmanship, the inventions kept flowing out of Brecknells. In 1954 the name of the company was changed to Brecknell, Dolman and Rogers, often shortened to BDR, reflecting the fact that Harry Dolman was the main decision maker. His policy of promoting keen young apprentices had paid off and new inventions were coming out of the drawing office - many of them variations of his original patents and others the ideas of the talented team he had put in place.

In 1948 he had been approached by an industrial chemist called H.E Meyer who had designed a laundry marking system, which he called Polymark. It applied special identification labels to garments by means of pressure and heat. The labels were porous so they remained on the garment during washing but could then be easily removed without leaving a trace.

Harry Dolman quickly saw the potential for the system and entered into a working relationship with Meyer and a company called Polymark Limited was formed. Brecknells designed a machine for its application and it soon became the main method of laundry marking in the UK - beating off all other systems, which had previously been imported into the country. Soon the laundry marking system was being exported to more than 70 countries worldwide. Polymark grew into a public company with subsidiary and agency companies in nearly every capital city in the world.

Under headlines such as: "New Bristol Machine Is A Dollar Winner" and "We've nothing like it, said Americans", the Evening World reported on how, in one visit to the USA and Canada, Harry

Dolman brought back orders worth at least a quarter of a million dollars a year.

The report quoted Harry Dolman saying: "We could have sold hundreds on the first day we exhibited in New York. I have now fixed an agent and I can promise brisk business." He also said that someone from the Bristol factory would have the opportunity to move to the USA to service the machines.

The packaging machines also got faster and faster, and on the same trip Harry Dolman made substantial sales of butter wrapping machines to the Canadians. The latest machines were able to pack more than double the number of sugar and butter packs in the same period of time. They were complicated machines and soon became firmly established on world markets. The first models developed for butter packaging could pack 54 bricks per minute. Developments over the decade saw four new models brought to the market so that eventually they were packing 220 packs per minute. The same machines were then developed for packing granulated sugar and flour.

The company became a major player in the vending machine business, which meant setting up a vending machine servicing organisation that had 160 vans equipped as travelling workshops that could drive around and make repairs even in the dead of night.

Household brand names, such as Tate and Lyle sugar, were using Brecknells' packaging machines. Major cigarette brands and confectionery brands, such as Cadbury, Fry, Nestle and Rowntree, were among those using the coin-operated vending machine.

Coin mechanisms were being used to operate other services such as luggage lockers, toilets, parking meters and stamp machines for the General Post Office. It was almost impossible not to encounter a machine in daily life that Harry Dolman had not somehow been involved in producing.

At one London press conference Harry unveiled the Vendol machine, which he described as an "automatic shop" - foreseeing a day when people would buy many goods from one vending machine rather than enter a shop. The newspaper report from the time says the machine would sell for £250 and paints a picture of how it worked and how it might be used.

The Bristol Evening Post report reads: "Called the Vendol it has 250 compartments of different sizes, perpetually revolving slowly round a central column. It revolves by friction only and therefore cannot go wrong through mishandling.

"In theory each of the 250 compartments could contain a different type of article - ranging from nylons, hair tonic, soft drinks or tinned soup to cigarettes, sweets or fruit.

"It will take 2s., 1s. or 6d. and, in each compartment, the appropriate change is sitting by the article. For instance, I put in 2s. and, when I opened the little door opposite the compartment of my choice I found 10 cigarettes and 2 and a half d.

"The Vendol, which is now going into production, has no comparable rival in the world at the moment I understand. It is 6ft. tall and a little over 2ft. square and will probably be used mainly on very large railway stations, piers and in canteens.

"The six-column machine - 3ft. tall and about 2ft. 6ins wide - takes 3d. or 6d. It displays its goods very clearly through Georgian wired glass which Mr Timmins (A. E Timmins who was managing director of the British Automatic Company, customer and collaborator with Brecknells) told me: "acts as a psychological as well as actual deterrent" to anybody who thinks of breaking into the machine.

"Mr Dolman told me that "quite a large order" for the Vendol had been made by one cinema circuit, also by the British Automatic Company."

Harry Dolman kept to his ideas about management and wherever possible promoted from within so that those who worked at the businesses could climb a ladder from apprentice to management in the same way that he did, engendering real loyalty within the workforce. By the 1960s every director on the board had been with the company all of their working lives.

The team at Brecknells worked hard and played hard and their talisman chairman was always playing a full part in the social scene. Fancy dress parties were frequently held; every kind of sporting competition was participated in with Brecknells having teams in local leagues.

Harry Dolman would be there to bowl skittles down a skittle alley dressed in feather boa, dark glasses and a cap; he'd be at the Christmas family get-together dressed as Father Christmas and handing out presents to the children; he would referee the football matches; captain a quiz team; lead the sing-songs and be one of the first to strut his stuff on the dance floor at an annual dinner-dance.

There was a management and a workers canteen at Brecknells and it was regarded as a great privilege to have made it into the management ranks and to be sitting at a table with Mr Dolman and senior management discussing the latest machines and inventions.

Brecknell, Dolman and Rogers were now "precision engineers" according to all their literature - and it was no idle boast. The products they were producing were leading the world and soon a third of total production was being exported and skilled men from the works were being sent all over the world to give advice, service and training to the overseas customers.

Harry was among those travelling the world and he joined other Brecknell international globe-trotters in getting a vaccination against smallpox in October 1952 in a bid to protect himself while travelling to some of the more exotic locations.

By the late 1950s the company was boasting that it was selling products in "nearly every country of the world" and its product list included packaging machines, egg grading machines, ticket issuing and change giving machines, weighing devices, printing presses, laundry marking machines, ice cream freezers and vending machines.

An exhibition was held showcasing local businesses at Whitchurch, on the site of the old airport where Harry had unsuccessfully tried to take off in the Flying Flea. Brecknell, Dolman and Rogers had a major stand at the show and attracted crowds by telling them this was where you could see: "How your sugar is packed, untouched by hand, on the fastest machine in the world; how your butter and margarine is hygienically packed; how your eggs are tested, counted, stamped and graded and then put into cartons; how your laundry is marked with a mark you never see; an exhibition of printing of high quality; a full range of coin operated vending machines including the "Vendol" automatic shop."

The success meant Harry Dolman's personal wealth was rising all the time and as well as travelling on business he took time out to travel for pleasure. He had a long term woman friend, although still living at the family home, described by his own daughter as "very glamorous and like a film star".

Harry was still having ideas for machines, scribbling them down on bits of cardboard and paper and anything that came to hand and then working them up into viable propositions on his drawing board at home - sometimes passing the ideas into the drawing office at Brecknells for others to develop.

But his big passion was now Bristol City and just a few years after the joy of promotion the club was staring relegation in the face and, in January 1958, by "mutual agreement", the manager Pat Beasley left the club.

Without anyone to select the team Harry sat down with trainer Les Bardsley and picked the side for the next game, making several changes and putting into practice some of his football theory. The side promptly lost 4-0 away to Leyton Orient.

He turned to the man he had wanted as manager eight years before, Peter Docherty, who had just resigned from Doncaster Rovers, who were also struggling at the bottom of the same division. Docherty was a great talker and tactician and wanted lots of changes in the dressing room. Harry Dolman was keen to let the new manager run the dressing room in his professional way, without interference from the board. He explained:

"One director we had used to go in at full time and make some remark when we had lost – "hard luck boys" - even when they had lost badly. He should have been telling the players that some of them deserved to have their wages stopped. The manager asked me to stop these visits, which of course I did.

"I have been in the dressing room on the odd occasion at half time when players have been cursing and swearing at each other. On other occasions, when the manager has been doing the cursing and other times when there has been five or six trainers, scouts and other members of the staff all giving private advice in little groups.

"The best and only way at half time is for the manager to get the players together. That is the time when managers can really show their worth.

"All teams have bad games sometimes and players, even when there is a good team spirit, know it is better, in my opinion for directors to keep away. When this happens players would rather have the whole thing forgotten until the heat is off.

"It was a practice at one time to send down to the dressing room champagne, beer, sherry or some other drink after matches. Peter

Docherty asked for this to be stopped. He pointed out that young players started to drink quite soon enough, without encouragement from the top. I agreed with the view, so for years we did not send any intoxicating drinks to the dressing room.

"We sent a good supply of ham sandwiches instead. Then, to my surprise, I heard that a certain new director had sent the players some champagne after they had won a cup tie. When I mentioned the matter to him he said he was paying for it himself. I said it is not a question of who pays for it, but a question of policy and whether it was good to encourage the players to drink, especially the young ones. However, this new director and others with him continued to break this rule and the cost of the drink was booked to the club. I was not against the club paying as opposed to directors, but I still think that, except on very special occasions, drink should be kept out of the dressing room."

Docherty kept the club in the Second Division that season, signing Bert Tindill from his old club, injecting new life into the team. Harry Dolman had always admired his footballing methods, which he had demonstrated at international level as manager of Northern Ireland, where he had led the unfashionable nation to the quarter finals of the World Cup, and gave him free reign to organise things his way at Bristol City. If Peter Docherty recommended a player then Harry Dolman backed his manager's judgement and tried to bring that player in. The aim was to get out of the Second Division at the top and realise the dream of playing in the First Division.

City fan Tom Hopegood said: "Although the records show that Peter Docherty was appointed by a board meeting there is no doubt that, in those days, Harry called all the shots. They used to joke that if there was a show of hands there was a leaver he pulled and all the hands shot up.

"I was told he wheeled Peter Docherty out of the tea room and introduced him to the board saying: "gentlemen meet the new manager of Bristol City". The rest of the board were all shocked to see him there. It was a bold move but Docherty never really had the dressing room.

"At the end of the season he called in Cyril Williams and other established players and got rid of them. He kept bringing in players from Doncaster as well as Irish players he knew. In the first months of 1958 suddenly there were whispers around that there were problems in the dressing room. There was even a talk of a religious divide with Protestant and Catholic players at loggerheads with the Irish influence. The season petered out and the team finished below half way in the table.

"That summer Docherty wanted to change the wage structure. He wanted to introduce a sliding scale so that players got different amounts depending on whether they were in the first team or not. John Atyeo, Mike Thresher and Tommy Burden went straight to Pennywell Road in John Atyeo's car to speak to Harry Dolman about it and say that they didn't like the way things were being done. Harry Dolman overrode the manager and insisted on keeping the wage structure, driving to Ashton Gate to talk to the manager."

The seeds of discontent had been sown and the 1959-60 season slid out of sight and following a disastrous 5-1 defeat at Brighton on March 12, Docherty was sacked. Once again Harry Dolman picked the side along with Les Bardsley and this time the team won 1-0 at home to Lincoln City.

It was a roller-coaster ride to the end of the season, but Bristol City finished bottom of the league with just 27 points. Relegation was confirmed in a 3-1 away defeat at Leyton Orient and Harry broke his own rule by buying champagne for the players to cheer them up on the way back to Bristol.

There have always been stories and rumours that some of City's wins in that period came about because Harry Dolman provided money to opposition players in brown envelopes. There is nothing in any of Harry's notes about the period to substantiate those rumours. Certainly he was passionate about Bristol City and desperate not to see them drop back down into the Third Division.

It was also clear that he wasn't used to making decisions that were later shown to be unsuccessful and having believed that Peter Docherty would bring success to the club, nobody could be more upset and disappointed. As Bristol City slumped down the table at the end of that year it took its toll on Harry Dolman and he became physically ill.

Johnny Watkins, one player who was sold by Docherty at the beginning of that season, hearing that a biography of Harry Dolman was being written, got in touch to tell his story.

He said: "Things certainly weren't good under Peter Docherty. I learned that I was being put on the transfer list by a note left in the dressing room. I remember being totally shocked and going to John Atyeo to tell him about it. I wanted to play for Bristol City but I ended up being transferred to Cardiff for £2,500.

"The next season I helped Cardiff to promotion while City were relegated. A few years later Harry Dolman took me aside one day, when I was at Ashton Gate watching a game, and said: "If I had known then what I know now you would never have been sold". He said that if I ever needed any help I was to get in touch with him.

"After my playing career ended I found myself out of work and he heard about it and gave me a job at Brecknell, Dolman and Rogers where I worked for 20 years. On my first day there I was shocked to see so many other ex-players and people from Bristol City - he had given them all jobs to help them out. Harry was always a good guy and a gentleman."

Harry had his own account of providing work for former players:

"I got to know the players very well. Some of them worried about their future – an injury sometimes would double the worry. Some clubs had no compunction about their players at the end of playing days. I helped a large number by training them to do a job. I gave many players a job at my factory and I also gave managers a job who had fallen on hard times. This is why I think men in large businesses are the most suitable people to be directors of football clubs, although I will agree that the modern footballer is better able to look after himself and the Football League helps them much more now than in my early days in the game.

"Another thing I did was to have everyone belonging to our club out to my house just before the season opened. They were given a good meal and games were organised and prizes presented to winners. This helped to create a good team spirit and managers liked me doing it.

"I also organised several trips abroad and in those days, because the club was so short of money, I made sure a profit from the trip would result.

"Times have changed in this respect now. Teams go abroad and almost invariably make a loss which the club has to meet. Directors go, have a good time, and couldn't care less about the cost. I think football clubs are the most unbusinesslike businesses I know of."

That unbusinesslike business had left Bristol City £55,000 in debt and Harry Dolman succumbed to his illness and was admitted to St Mary's Private Hospital in Clifton, Bristol. His team had been relegated just a few short years after "the best day of his life" but his business was thriving and he was a wealthy and successful man - just feeling the strain a little at 63-years-old.

The Board of Directors met without him in May but were

astonished to hear from vice chairman Bill Kew that he had a message from Harry, who had promised to clear the complete debt. The story sent shockwaves around the world of football and sent the headline writers into overdrive.

The News Chronicle opened its column with the words: "Who is this man Harry Dolman...this man with the Midas touch...this man who could afford to give away £55,000?"

Harry told the newspaper: "I know people will say I have more money than sense - but I don't care a damn. Frankly, I am now a rich man. I could have retired before the war and still be living comfortably. This is my way of enjoying my wealth. I hope to see Bristol City rise to the top.

"I don't have to work now. But I like it. I have made my money in Bristol and giving some of it to the club is one way of showing appreciation to the city. As I lay in the nursing home last week I thought of giving the club a loan. But the club would still be paying the money back after I was dead. So I might as well give the money while I am alive.

"Ever since I joined the board 21 years ago the club has been saddled with debts. Now perhaps we can forget about money and concentrate on success."

What Harry Dolman actually handed to Bristol City was not a wedge of cash but more than 25,000 four shilling units in Brecknell, Dolman and Rogers stock, which put the club back on a firm financial footing and made a direct connection between his outside business success and Bristol City. He also insisted on a shake-up of the boardroom with two directors, George Jones, who had been on the board for 11 years, and the Reverend Frederick Vyvyan-Jones leaving. He wanted other safeguards in return for his generosity.

Harry gave an account of that period of his life:

"Promotion in 1955 was, of course, a great day for me and if we had spent some money on the right players we could have gone on up. We were, in fact, on top of the league about Christmas, looking certain, but injuries and loss of form due mainly, in my opinion, to an ageing team, soon put paid to our chances and three years later we again went back to the third Division.

"This made me really ill for the first time in my life. In fact I had to go to a nursing home for a major operation and whilst I was there the bank closed on the club. We had an overdraft of about £60,000. Something had to be done quickly.

"I had recovered from my operation and was convalescing when I heard the news. We could have sold a player. Big John Atyeo was the envy of many clubs, but top transfer fees were only in the region of £25,000. He was the only asset we had and if we sold him it would only be a third of what we required, but I had promised I would not sell our best players and the board were all agreed on this policy. Furthermore, I had promised John's father that he would never be transferred. He hated the transfer system.

"However, no-one had any solution to this problem and when eventually the matter was brought to me officially by the vice chairman, I told him I would pay the club's debts and lent them £30,000 interest free, providing (a) they gave me the deeds whilst the club owed me money and (b) providing two directors would resign. I do not want or intend to go into the reasons for asking for the resignation of the two directors, but for the club's sake they agreed and I carried out my promise to pay the clubs debts in full.

"Soon after that I loaned the club the £30,000 interest free and asked for the deeds to be handed over whilst this money was owing. Much to my surprise, and annoyance the legal director was very reluctant to let me have these. They had, of course, been taken from the bank and were at his office. As I had cleared the overdraft and given the club something in the region of £60,000, it seemed strange that he was willing for the bank to have the deeds, but not me. All other members of the board were on my side so I just told him to bring them in, which he did. This is another case of strange ideas by individual directors.

"The loan was returned in two years and the deeds handed back to the club and it wasn't long before they were back in the bank as security to the bank for another overdraft. We were far from paying our way and if it had not been for the money the supporters club were getting in on pools, we should have been in bankruptcy. This state of affairs continued until the end of my period of office as chairman. We were still spending a great deal of money on the ground, terracing, lavatory accommodation, turnstiles, fencing in the Covered End and barriers. For many years all we had for seating was a wooden shed on the east side. This shed held about 900 spectators. It was condemned by the planning authorities and if I hadn't sent my own men from B.D.R. to strengthen and make other extensive repairs, we could not have used it."

The club was back on an even financial footing so the next thing to do was to appoint a manager. This time Harry chose Fred Ford, a coach at Bristol Rovers. Ford had learned his craft as a trainer under the legendary Bill Shankly and had a growing reputation in the game. At first he refused to make the switch across Bristol but after a few conversations with Harry Dolman signed a three-year contract. His mission was to get Bristol City back into Division Two as quickly as possible.

Now back in full health the legendary Harry Dolman smile and cigar pose returned as he looked forward to brighter days. It was affairs of the heart, though, which were to bring the next major event of his life.

MARINA

Marina Crossley was born in Hong Kong in 1936 where her father was serving in the military. Her childhood involved attending seven different schools as her family moved around the country following her father. Soon after the war the family moved to Bristol and after leaving Merrywood Girls' School Marina attended the Phyllis Christie private secretarial college in Cheltenham where she learned shorthand, typing and other skills.

She said: "One of the lessons was called 'boss management' and was all about how to handle the boss when you are a secretary - that came in very handy later! By 1959 I was working as a secretary/ translator in Hanover, Germany, and really went there to improve my German language skills.

"I had applied to be an air hostess with BOAC but on returning to England my mother became ill and wanted me to move back to Bristol to be near her."

It was her mother who spotted an advertisement in the Bristol Evening Post for a managing director's secretary in Bristol that required not only secretarial skills but knowledge of French and German. It wasn't the sort of job Marina was looking for but to please her mother she sent off an application.

Said Marina: "I really didn't want the job. I had plans to go to London as I had been accepted by BOAC, subject to interview, to be a stewardess. I really wanted a job travelling. The advertisement invited applications to a PO Box number, so I didn't know who the job was with. This was in July 1959 and I wrote a very nonchalant letter stating that my contract with a German company did not cease until October 31, but if the position wasn't filled, after that I was available. It was very off-hand and I was convinced that would be the last I would hear and I really only wrote the application to please my mother."

The job was as secretary to Harry Dolman who needed a secretary with language skills to cope with the growing international business. A copy of his reply to Marina on September 4, 1959, still exists.

It reads: "In reply to your letter of 31st August, the vacancy for a Secretary may not be filled by the time you return to Bristol and if you are still interested perhaps you will come to see me as early as possible."

It wasn't what the young Marina wanted to hear at all. She tried to put off the interview but in November 1959 she travelled back from Germany and at 11am on November 6 she met Harry Dolman for the first time in his office at Pennywell Road.

Marina remembers it as a very long and thorough interview during which Harry Dolman talked about aspects of the job, how it was essential to keep confidences, as the secretary would be privy to lots of confidential information, and he then tested her shorthand skills.

She said: "I shall never forget that test. It was a really horrible piece of technical jargon and engineering terminology, but fortunately I was quite good at shorthand, and I was able to read it back to him.

"He explained to me how busy he was; how he needed a personal secretary and how it would mean dealing with his personal correspondence. He explained about his role at Bristol City Football Club and said that the job had a salary of £10 a week.

"I said that the job advertisement had said that a knowledge of French and German was required and with those extra skills I would expect £12 a week. He called in the company secretary and said to him: "This is Miss Crossley, she wants £12 a week and I've said she can have it."

"The company secretary said that the plan was for £10 a week but if that was what Mr Dolman wanted then so be it. That was how I found myself working as Harry Dolman's private secretary."

Fifteen months later Marina married Harry Dolman. He was 63 and she was 24 at the time of their wedding.

For the first year as his secretary it was strictly business. She worked at dictation and letter-writing and all the 101 tasks that secretaries were expected to perform in those days before the desktop computer. But, in November 1960, director and Company Secretary Stewart Redfern was suffering from bronchitis and was unable to do the work required following eight board meetings.

Harry asked Marina to help out and she spent long hours going through the paperwork, sometimes in the office until 7pm.

She said: "Harry left the office at 4pm to attend outside meetings and that was my opportunity to settle down to the extra work."

As a reward for her dedicated work he invited her out for dinner. A bond began to develop between them and the relationship became much friendlier with a shared sense of humour and fun. On January 28 Stewart Redfern died. It was sudden and unexpected and routines in the business had to change.

Marina took his place opening the post with Harry and one morning there was a letter to Harry that mentioned marriage to him, which made them both laugh.

Marina takes up the story: "As we were laughing Harry just started to talk about marriage and said to me: "Would you marry me if I asked you?" I laughed at the idea as I thought it was a joke and just said: "Yes, of course". He looked me straight in the eye and said: "Would you really, Marina? think about it", and I looked at him and thought "Oh my goodness he means it!"

"We changed the subject and he didn't mention it again during the following week and I thought maybe I had imagined his seriousness.

But then he spoke to me again and we decided to talk about it. We talked and talked and I finally said yes, it would work very well."

Marina and Harry knew that with the age gap of 39 years, and with his position in society as the very wealthy boss of a successful business and his profile as chairman of Bristol City, tongues were likely to wag and the media would certainly be taking an interest.

Marina said: "We kept talking about it and discussed what people would say about the age difference. Then one day he was at a football league meeting in London and he rang me and said that he didn't think getting married would be fair to me as I was too young. He said that at the weekend he would be back in Bristol and we should talk about it then; I thought then that it wouldn't happen.

"The following week I had some time off and was going to go to Wales but we decided to talk about it properly and he drove us to Portland Bill in Dorset. We got there at 12pm and just sat on the rocks for four hours and we talked and talked about what people would say, how I would be accused of being a gold-digger, what they would say about him and whether we were both strong enough to face the critics. We decided to go ahead."

Harry Dolman was still living in the same house as his first wife, and in April 1961 he applied for the decree nisi and a special licence to marry Marina on April 15. After living separate lives, albeit under the same roof, for 15 years, Harry moved out to start a new life with his young secretary.

Of course, marrying a woman who was younger than his daughter, Hazel, was always bound to raise eyebrows and understandably some difficulties in the family. But in time Marina developed a good relationship with Harry's children and he always ensured his first wife and children were looked after.

The ceremony was held at 9.30am at Bristol Register Office in front of just a few close friends and Marina's family. Then they went to the Grand Hotel in Bristol for a small reception. As they left, newspaper photographers and reporters were gathered outside and Harry's Rolls Royce, registration HD 11, was taken around the back to smuggle them out.

One reporter spotted them making their getaway and jumped on to the running board of the car - it was Marina's first glimpse of what life would be like as the glamorous young wife of a business tycoon and football club chairman.

She said later: "My parents were not very happy about it, and said I was wasting my life. It might sound like a cliché, but Harry was my soul-mate and once we had decided there was no point in waiting. No one knew in advance but it caused uproar as soon as news got out.

"I probably married an older man because I spent my early childhood, before my younger sister came along, living with much older people. My mother was one of eight, and I was very spoilt as the baby of the family with uncles and aunts who used to take me out; it meant I grew up finding other people my own age rather immature.

"I think the age gap between Harry and me seemed more like 20 years than nearly 40, because in those days I was older than my years and he was younger than his. Never for one moment did I regret my decision and I know he didn't.

"He was a wonderful dancer, very light on his feet. At the Brecknells social he and the other directors wore Tutus and sang "Tiptoe Through The Tulips". We loved dancing together and Harry always played tennis and table tennis and we had some wonderful holidays together as well as a good working relationship."

On the day Harry and Marina married three American-built bombers attacked the main Cuban air force base near Havana, in a move that was to build to the Cuban Missile Crisis the following year. That was the main news on the front of the Bristol Evening Post but "Mr Harry Dolman Weds Secretary" was the second most important story of the day.

Marina and Harry escaped the madness of the media by going to the Savoy Hotel in London and then to Nice in the South of France and then on to Venice, and just let the tongues wag at home while they enjoyed their honeymoon. Returning to Bristol they lived in a small flat at the Grand Spa Hotel, Clifton, while they looked for a home.

A house at Chew Magna had recently been sold by Lady Wills, part of the cigarette dynasty well-known to Harry. The man who had bought it intended to do some work on it but shortly after returning from honeymoon Marina and Harry visited the house and within 20 minutes Harry Dolman had made an offer and bought the impressive property.

Said Marina: "After a quick look around Harry turned to me and said: "Would you like this house?" Of course it was beautiful but there was so much garden and 13 acres of land attached to it so my first reaction was to question the size of it and knowing how much Harry hated gardening, who was actually going to keep it up together.

"He simply said: "oh we can get someone else to look after the garden" and with that the decision was made. He was right, of course, and we had four fields that we let out for local grazing. We had been married in April 1961 and on August 4 we moved into this lovely house.

"Of course we had been living in flats so we had no furniture and at first it was a little creepy there, especially in the evening when Harry was not around. The first day we were there Harry went into Bristol to play Bridge with his friends, which he did most Friday nights, and I was left alone.

"Boards were creaking and it felt very echoey and lonely and as the night drew on I became frightened. The time for Harry to arrive back came and went and there was no sign of him. A few hours went by and I was getting more and more scared. Suddenly I saw headlights on the driveway and Harry arrived back. He was late because he had got lost in the lanes around Chew Magna, after taking a wrong turn in the dark and had spent a couple of hours trying to find his own house!"

Now in his early sixties Harry had notched back a little on his office hours and only worked at Brecknells from 10am to 4pm. He set about making improvements to his new home - but as usual they were all mechanical and practical and he created his own workshop.

He took down the stable clock, which had been keeping erratic time for more than a hundred years, dismantled it all over his workshop floor and then built entirely new works for it, with five ratchet wheels and an electric motor, so that it then kept perfect time.

He built his own firedogs for several rooms in the house, designing, welding and cutting the metal himself and putting the whole fireplace on casters so that it could be wheeled out for the ashes to be emptied and for it to be restocked with logs.

No less than 10 chandeliers were bought for the house and, of course, Harry decided to hang them himself - with Marina's help.

Said Marina: "The biggest one Harry decided we should hang after Sunday lunch one day. He was up in the loft void pulling on ropes and I was down below guiding it. Suddenly we realised that the rope was fraying and I shouted up and he just about managed to lower it before the last thread of rope snapped.

"I said we shall have to get a professional in. Harry was in a sweat at the effort and decided to take a bath. By the time he had got out of the bath he said he had an idea and he rigged the ropes differently and within 20 minutes the job was done. Somehow he had worked out a way for just the two of us to do something that the experts said would take four people - that was typical of Harry."

Within two years the seven-bedroom Regency House had been transformed into a home fit for a wealthy tycoon and his young bride. They had their own bowling green in the grounds - where Harry invited teams of Bristol Rovers and Bristol City directors to compete against each other; they had a games room with a full-sized billiard table where Harry challenged his fellow board members from Brecknell, Dolman and Rogers to games and Marina had her own sewing room and got used to living the life of a football club owner.

Beautiful French-style furniture was purchased for the lounge, which had a large portrait of Harry over the main fireplace. Soon it was the subject of magazine articles as Harry enjoyed the fruits of his labours over the years.

The house and garden became a full-time project for Marina, whose role was now to run the home and accompany Harry as his wife, and she stood down from her role in the business.

One of the first events where they appeared together in public as man and wife was the dinner and dance to celebrate the creation of a new cricket club for Brecknell, Dolman and Rogers. Marina was presented with a bouquet of flowers and Harry praised the founders of the club, Dave Western, Mike Barnes, Colin Lewis and Bill Tovey, but said: "It is about time we had a bowling club. We old people play bowls and I think we should have a bowling club at Brecknells." He brought along former Bristol City goalkeeper Bob Anderson as a guest.

Marina's life had been transformed and she now found herself at all sorts of functions and, of course, that also meant getting involved in Bristol City Football Club.

Marina initially thought her Saturdays would be free while Harry went to watch football but he asked her to accompany him to Ashton Gate and to look after the directors wives, who were not allowed in the boardroom but had their own room at that time. This often included the wives and female friends of visiting directors.

Every other Saturday she would watch the reserves playing in the combination league. But one day there was a major game against Bournemouth and Harry asked Fred Ford if Marina could travel on the team coach and he said, "Yes, of course".

Marina said: I felt a little embarrassed on boarding the coach as I was the only woman. To make matters worse we had only got as far as Newton St Loe when I realised I wanted to spend a penny. There were no toilets on the coaches in those days and Harry was busy chatting to other directors further back in the coach. I went to ask him discretely but he was too busy and just said: "Control yourself we can't stop yet".

"Fred Ford, who had been sitting at the front, came up through the coach a few minutes later to make sure everyone was comfortable. When I explained my difficulty he was wonderful. In a short while the coach pulled into a pub car park and he announced that we would have a comfort break if anyone wanted one.

"Of course this never usually happened and I was the only one who trooped off the coach to the pub toilet and ran the gauntlet of player whispers when I returned to my seat!"

Being the wife of a football club chairman did bring some memorable days, though. Bristol-born movie star Cary Grant often stayed at the Grand Spa Hotel overlooking Avon Gorge, which was also a place where Harry and Marina knew the management well.

One day Cary Grant told the hotel he would really like to go to a football match while he was in Bristol and the request was passed to Harry, who arranged for him to be picked up from the hotel, have lunch at his home in Chew Magna before travelling in HD11 to Ashton Gate.

The visit was a complete secret and the Hollywood legend, who had appeared alongside Mae West, Audrey Hepburn, Grace Kelly and Rita Hayworth, duly arrived with his glamorous wife Dyan Cannon, herself a screen legend.

The Grants and the Dolmans had a nice meal and walked in the garden. Marina's sister asked if she could film Cary Grant and the star said that would be fine.

Marina said: "It was only for a little home movie but Cary Grant kept asking us what we wanted him to do and how he should pose. It seemed he was used to having direction when he was being filmed and my sister and I giggled at this big star asking us what he should do on camera."

As they set off from the Chew Valley in Harry's Rolls-Royce Cary Grant said he was worried that he might be recognised and besieged by autograph hunters and Harry reassured him that he had a parking place close to the entrance so few people were likely to notice him. As the Rolls Royce pulled into Ashton Gate through the Ashton Park entrance some young lads ran up to the car with pens and autograph books and Cary Grant said: "Oh, here we go. They have spotted us."

Cary was sitting behind Harry, who was driving, and Marina was asked to jump out and dash around and open the door to protect the film star. But the fans ran past Cary Grant and said "Mr Dolman could we have your autograph please", at which Cary Grant laughed and said: "That shows me." Cary Grant and Dyan Cannon happily entered the football ground unnoticed while their host signed autographs in the car park.

It was the first of a small number of visits by the star to Ashton Gate and, after his complaint on the first occasion that there was no popcorn or food to be had while watching the game, as there was in baseball and American football, Marina popped to the local shops to ensure he had a tin of popcorn by his seat - among the first catering ever offered at Ashton Gate.

Marina and Harry had a very successful marriage and her support for him and the football club was recognised by Bristol City Supporters Club who, following Harry's death, invited her to succeed him as their president in January 1978. In November 1997 she was invited to be Bristol City Club President and in January 2017 the walkway behind the new Lansdown Stand was named Marina Dolman Way in her honour.

THE SIXTIES

"Harry Dolman, the man who will go down in the annals of football as the greatest benefactor any club has ever had the fortune to possess, has dipped into his bank balance yet again to assist the club dearest to his heart."

The superlatives by the Evening Post's legendary sport's writer Peter Godsiff may seem a little over the top in the context of today's billionaire investments into football clubs across the world, but it shows just how important a further £15,000 loan that Harry Dolman made in August 1961 meant in Bristol.

Just four months into his new marriage, and while financing his new home in Chew Magna and its contents, Harry wiped out the club's bank overdraft to enable Fred Ford to start spending money on players and build the team that would take City into Division Two.

Harry and Fred Ford had tried to sign local boy and Bristol Rovers forward Alfie Biggs, but he had been sold to Preston, much to their disappointment.

Harry told Peter Godsiff at the start of the 1961-62 season: "If we can make a good start to this season, and it looks as if we have got a chance, we shall certainly go out to strengthen any weaknesses. The club won't hesitate to buy. I feel sure we shall do much better than last year.

"Much depends on our inside-forwards - whether they are up to expectations and can get goals. If the two young players, Bobby Williams and Brian Clark, come off we have got a bright future ahead of us.

"We should have liked to have signed Biggs or Hooper or both from Bristol Rovers. It is a pity such a good player as Biggs should have been allowed to leave Bristol - I believe the Bristol Rovers chairman said the same thing - particularly as Bristol City wanted the player and were willing to negotiate for him. We did make a substantial offer, as you know.

"But it may prove to be a blessing in disguise for it gives young Clark a wonderful opportunity to establish himself.

"We knew all about the capabilities of Biggs and Hooper- Fred Ford did, more than anybody - and Fred was keen to bring them here. If an opportunity arose for similar players, we should certainly give close consideration to making an offer.

"Now we are starting a new season we feel we must give the young boys a chance. If we could solve our player problems with local boys, then we would rather it that way - and I think the supporters would agree with us."

Fred Ford himself was under no illusions at the task ahead. In a newspaper column at the start of that same season he said: "Everyone here on the staff earns his wages. There has been first class co-operation from the players and they will do their best according to their ability.

"They train hard and there is discipline within the club. The club is greater than the individual. If it turns out that I cannot improve on last season's work then I can be treated the same as a player who has not lived up to expectations. I read in a Sunday newspaper last weekend that if Bristol City finish under 14th I will resign. I have never spoken to the reporter concerned though he reads my articles.

"Whether or not money is spent has little to do with it - this club has always been prepared to have a gamble on an overdraft."

In fact Fred Ford's second season in charge saw Bristol City finish sixth in the table, signs that with some sound management both on and off the field a little progress was being made. It took

The Board of Directors at Bristol City Football Club photographed at the ground on March 2, 1953. Harry is seated in the middle of the front row.

September 1954: Harry accepts a cheque for £4,000 from the Chairman of the 51 Club, Mr Cecil Colston. The executive supporters club was a handy source of funds for Bristol City FC.

Harry finally gets his man and welcomes Peter Docherty as manager of
Bristol City FC during the BBC programme 'Roundays' on June 28, 1958.

With the floodlights that Harry designed in the distance, the Ashton Gate
pitch gets an overhaul in May 1959. Between May 6 and 13, 5,000 tons
of soil was hauled and spread over the pitch. The ground staff then laid turf
that was supplied from Cumberland.

As well as Football League games, in April 1965 Ashton Gate hosted the
Gloucestershire Youth Cup Final, with Bedminster Down Boys' Club beating
Kingswood Youth Club 2-1. The stand in the background would soon be
demolished to make way for the Dolman Stand.

The men who try to do something and fail
are definitely better than those who try to do
nothing and succeed.

Harry Dolman compiled a photograph album about his beloved Brecknells. The volume started with one of his management philosophies, reproduced above top. Within the pages Harry is seen in all sorts of guises, including playing Father Christmas at the company's 1955 children's party, presenting trophies to glamorous employees, and appearing in fancy dress with fellow directors at a Brecknells function.

Top left: a poster inviting potential customers and members of the public to come along to stand number 248 at Whitchurch in July 1958. Bottom left shows some of the BDR products on display at the show, including cigarette and chocolate vending machines. Special attention was drawn to the 'Vendol' Automatic Shop that would vend anything wrapped or unwrapped within its size or price range. Another part of the stand contained a fully working egg grading machine and a butter packing machine. Top right: a BDR poster making the point that the company's products were, by the end of the 1950s, in use all over the world, thanks in the main to Harry's inventive mind, his drive and tenacity.

Top left: a bank of BDRs London Underground ticket machines. Top right: a postage stamp dispensing machine. Bottom: Queen Elizabeth II is introduced to Harry at the Dairy Show held at Olympia, London, in 1964. Harry went on to show the Queen a display of BDR products.

Roulette

The first Automatic Roulette Table ever made is now installed in the Squash Lounge at Ashton Court Country Club and is operating continuously.

It was invented by Mr. Harry Dolman and was produced by Brecknell, Dolman & Rogers after many years of intensive experiments.

The stakes are 6d, 1/- and 2/-. We hope that members and guests will enjoy using the machine.

Late 1960s and a prototype of Harry's Roulette machine gets its first airing at Ashton Court Country Club. Harry, back centre with trademark cigar in hand, can be seen playing the game enthusiastically.

Top: the BDR designed Polymark laundry marking system became the main method of laundry marking in the UK and was exported to more than 70 countries. Middle: one of BDRs Sealtite flour packing machines in service at Junction Mills in Scotland. Bottom right: Harry became President of the Bristol Incorporated Chamber of Commerce and Shipping in 1966. Bottom left: in 1968, BDRs success led to the company receiving the Queen's Award to Industry for Technological Innovation in the manufacture of Food Packaging Machinery. In 1970, Harry received the OBE for Services to Export.

Top: Harry and Marina about to board a plane at Lulsgate Airport to visit Cork with a delegation from the Bristol Chamber of Commerce in 1966. Bottom: Harry and Marina aboard the RMS Queen Elizabeth on their way to New York in 1965.

Harry's first Rolls Royce Silver Cloud with Commissionaire Jack Nutt (a great City supporter) and Bob, the Chauffeur. The '11' in the registration plate stood for the 11 players in a football team.

The 1964-65 promotion winners. Back row (left to right): Brian Thurlow, Jack Connor, Mike Gibson, 'Chuck' Drury, Gordon Low. 2nd row (left to right): Les Bardsley, Harry Dolman, Alec Briggs, Steve Stacey, Terry Bush, Bobby Etheridge, Mike Thresher, Tony Ford, Fred Ford (Manager), Arthur Proudler. 3rd row (left to right): Jantzen Derrick, Brian Clarke, John Ateyo, Bobby Williams, Ray Savino, Peter Hooper. Front row (left to right): 'Lou' Peters, Gerry Sharpe, Gordon Parr.

Harry welcomes Bristol City's new manager, Alan Dicks, to Ashton Gate in 1967.

• Board give go-ahead

£50,000 STAND FOR 5,000 BY 1968

Minister praises Dolman Stand

Work starts next week on City's stand— at £220,000

too late. "I feel we are providing a valuable amenity for the city of Bristol and, anyway, our club is a great asset to Bristol."

City put up ticket prices

Stand cash battle is almost won

City trim pitch for new stand

Press clippings from the late 1960s as Harry's dream of a new stand gets plenty of press coverage. Some things never change!

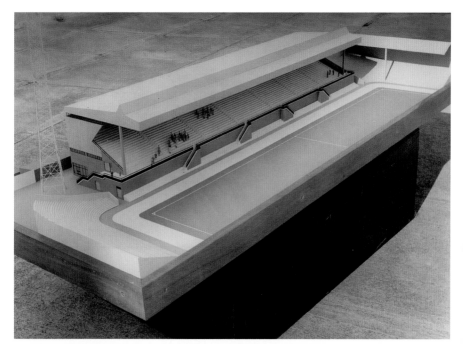

Top: the model that Harry built, showing his design for the new stand. Bottom: Harry's plans being put into effect. Nearing completion, in June 1970, Harry holds a site meeting with Bill Needham-Cooper and Ronald Kendall, of Tube Construction Ltd, and Alan Dicks.

Pretty much everyone involved in Bristol City Football Club is in this framed picture presented by the Bristol Evening Post on December 16, 1970, to mark the club's entry into the semi-final of the Football League Cup. The photo was taken from the newly completed Dolman Stand towards what is now the Lansdown Stand.

In front of the stand on the far side are two mounted policemen who used to be on duty at every home match; in the back row are Supporters' Club officials, Arthur Fowler, Beryl Fudge, Mary Andrews, Jim Evans and Chris Janes. Secretary Bert Bush, manager's secretary Anne Thomason, financial secretary Tony Sully. Groundsmen Norman Jennings, Mike Lillington and Fred Shaw. Promotions and development team of June Weaver, Ted Packer and Marion McClusky. In front of them, in the next row, are the club's apprentice professionals, including a young Len Bond, and in front of them are Harry Dolman with his fellow directors and club doctors, Dennis Fowler and John Andrews. The next row sees Terry Bush with reserve team players in white, including Keith Fear, Tom Ritchie and Ray Cashley. In front of them are the physio, manager and coaches before the front three rows comprising the first team squad. City legends such as Geoff Merrick, Trevor Jacobs, Chris Garland, John Galley, David Rodgers, Trevor Tainton, Ken Wimshurst and Alan Skirton are all in view and the skipper, holding the ball, is Dickie Rooks.

Top: now president of the club, Harry Dolman celebrates with the crowd after the historic win against Portsmouth that secured the club's return to the top flight of English Football for the first time in 65 years. Bottom: Harry celebrates with, right to left, goal scorer Clive Whitehead, Gerry Sweeney, Gerry Gow and Donnie Gillies.

EVENING POST

BRISTOL CITY

★ PROMOTION SPECIAL

"Say Cheese . . ." and here's the result, a section of the promotion-happy fans.

DIVISION ONE HERE WE COME

By PETER GODSIFF

They're up. Bristol City have made it back to the First Division after 65 years.

The 1—0 win over Portsmouth clinched it and ended the nervous anxiety, the heartaches and the worry of the last couple of months.

But it has been a 10-month struggle for the team and supporters.

Although the club had been in the top three since October 7 and led the table for two months until just before Easter, the doubts and uncertainty remained.

Would they fold up at the final hurdle? Would there be a repeat of last season's situation when they were all but there on Good Friday, but dropped three points out of four in the home games against Norwich and Rovers and fluffed it?

As the weeks passed and City showed no sign of faltering, the confidence of their followers increased.

Shielded

Manager Alan Dicks shielded his players as much as possible from the promotion glare.

Promotion talk was discouraged. Superstitions predominated.

The manager wore the same suit to each match; the players trotted out in the same order. They insisted on wearing the same numbered shirts.

Yet promotion looked decades away after 3-1 defeats in the first two away games at Hull and Southampton.

Amazingly — and significantly — the away form for the rest of the season tipped the balance City's way. They gathered 23 points from the other 19 games, suffered only three one-goal defeats.

The highlight, I believe, was the 4-2 win at Oldham on October 7 which took them into second spot. That night soccer celebrities paid glowing tributes to City.

But it was not a smooth ride. Paul Cheesley, who leapt to prominence with 11 goals in the first 13 matches, was injured on Boxing Day against Plymouth.

He was in and out of the side for several weeks, the team lost much of its momentum and performances suffered. This was the City's bad spell — but they got the results and survived.

The players began to get a touch of the jitters in home games, too. They were conscious of not producing their best.

A 1-1 draw against Southampton, a shock 2-0 home defeat by Nottingham Forest and a narrow 1-0 win over Oldham three days later were the three uneasy home games in February.

It was about then that Bolton and Sunderland — both involved in the FA Cup — started to lose points unexpectedly.

The pressure on them made City's third round Cup exit at Coventry one of the important results of the season.

The Cup defeat helped in another way, too. It enabled manager Dicks to persuade Plymouth to stage their Easter Saturday game at Home Park on January 24 instead. The goal-less draw was invaluable to City and relieved the congestion at Easter when the tension was at its height.

Tension

It was on March 6 when they cut loose with a 3-0 home win over Luton that they looked the part again.

The greatest result was the 1-0 win at West Bromwich followed by the 1-1 draw at Sunderland who equalised four minutes from time.

But it was still not over.

Defeat at Blackpool, a further home draw against Chelsea and just one point from the local derby on Good Friday kept the tension going right to the finish.

Then, Sunderland beat Bolton 2-1 on Easter Monday before 52,000 hysterical fans at Roker and just two points were required from the last two home matches.

Relegation-doomed Portsmouth provided the points — and the champagne flowed.

Against a background of flags and banners president Harry Dolman and manager Alan Dicks acknowledge the cheers of the crowd.

The Promotion Special produced by the Bristol Evening Post sees Harry Dolman and Alan Dicks celebrating with the fans after the match.

Top: in his 'retirement' Harry loved to play bowls, either at home in Chew Magna, at St Andrews Park in Bristol or here, at Page Park Bowling Club. Bottom: although now suffering ill health, Harry was still able to enjoy the company of City legends Arthur Milton, John Ateyo and Don Clark at his 80th birthday celebration in August 1977, just three months before he passed away. (Image courtesy George Gallop collection).

a few seasons, and the signing of some players, such as goalkeeper Mike Gibson and Gordon Parr, who worked at Brecknells, to build a strong side.

The 1964-65 season saw Bristol City competing at the top end of the Division Three table but the pressure was on Fred Ford and Harry Dolman as Bristol Rovers were front runners. They had brought Alfie Biggs back to Bristol and were flying high. So when Rovers came to Ashton Gate in February and City came out 2-1 winners there was something to celebrate.

Tom Hopegood said: "I heard that Harry Dolman was so keen to beat the Rovers that he handed £55 in an envelope to John Atyeo - £5 for each player - and said they would get it if they won! On the Monday he was back at Brecknells in Pennywell Road wearing a red carnation as a signal that the City had won. He walked around with a big beaming smile on his face.

"He always had a soft spot for Rovers really, but liked the banter and rivalry. One time when there was a union issue over a round of redundancies planned, Harry attended a meeting in the Brecknell's canteen. Someone shouted out to him: "Mr Dolman, can you tell us please, where do you think the cuts will come first?" Harry jokingly answered: "Well, if anyone in this room has a Bristol Rovers season ticket they will probably be first!" He could be very sharp, and a lot of fun."

Harry's money and Fred Ford's careful spending, team selection and tactics resulted in success when, in a nail-biting end to the 1964-65 season, Bristol City finished second on goal average above Mansfield Town to gain promotion back to the Second Division.

In the run-up to that promotion Daily Express sports reporter John Davies tracked the Dolman's down to the Colony Club in Barbados where they had flown after a rain-soaked game at St James Park, Exeter, speaking to Harry Dolman on the telephone.

His report quotes Harry Dolman saying: "Second division football is merely a minimum of ambition for Bristol City. I consider that division merely a springboard to the greater things both my club and Bristol, as a centre of soccer, really deserve."

The report goes on: "This was Chairman Dolman's theme as he spoke thousands of miles away from the humble surroundings of Blundell Park, Cleethorpes, where Bristol City battle tonight hoping to record their sixth win in a row against Grimsby.

"It is a game that also marks the 600th appearance of 33-year-old John Atyeo for Bristol City. "Wish the lads and Big John all the best from me," Dolman boomed over the line. "Remind them that when City won promotion 10 years ago we were undefeated in our last 18 games. Football can be a big seller in Bristol. I've known this for years but getting to the top is the hardest part of the job. Soccer is not like any other business. The best laid plans can go wrong through no one's fault. I promised that City would get promotion at the beginning of the season and I still think that our team will honour my pledge. Certainly after the recent run of success it would be crazy to write us off.

"As far as John Atyeo is concerned he's been a great servant to the club and I would like to see him mark this milestone in his career with our return to the Second Division. Whatever happens we shall spend something like £20,000 on new floodlighting at Ashton Gate this summer. But that will be merely a start to our development if we do clinch promotion. It is difficult for a club to plan too ambitiously from the basement of the Third and Fourth Divisions."

Such a tight season came right down to the wire with City having to beat Oldham Athletic at home on the last day in front of more than 28,000 supporters. The game ended in a 2-0 win and in the elation and euphoria of the result Harry promptly declared to Fred Ford at a directors banquet to celebrate promotion that he had "a job for life".

He also splashed out on a holiday in the South of France for Fred and his wife Pat; a £1,000 pay rise and a two-year extension to his contract. Harry Dolman was determined that this time the club would stay in the Second Division and push on further to reach the top flight.

His lifestyle now seemed lavish compared to the fans of the football club and the workers in his business. Driving around in his Rolls Royce with his young bride, disappearing for weeks on end to exotic locations for holidays with Marina and arriving late and leaving early from the business seemed to be the height of luxury to casual observers. In fact Harry was just enjoying the rewards that all his hard work and dedication over the years had brought him and he liked to play up to the image.

In fact he also owned a Mini car and was just as likely to take that out for a spin. He loved playing bowls, darts and Bridge - with his Friday night Bridge games among his favourite activities. He became president of St Andrew's Bowling Club as well as hosting games in his own garden. He also spent time and money supporting charities and good causes.

In 1960 he was one of the founding board members of the Industrial Therapy Organisation in Bristol. At that time an industrial therapy scheme had been pioneered by Dr. Donald Early at Glenside Hospital, Bristol, in an industrial unit that saw 400 long term psychiatric patients employed, regaining their confidence and self-assurance.

They were mostly working on assembling items, such as ballpoint pens and electrical components. Harry Dolman was a key member of the board that bought an old school premises and built it up as a factory to enable those with mental health problems to earn a living and then get jobs back in employment.

In the early days machinery from Brecknell, Dolman and Rogers was donated to the scheme and some patients were also offered roles at Brecknells. Harry served on the board for 12 years, by which time the wages paid annually to worker patients had reached £54,153. One of Harry's proudest moments was showing Princess Anne around a new Bristol workshop in 1969, when she visited to officially open it.

Harry and Marina loved putting on their finery to attend charity events, including star-studded dinners with the Variety Club of Great Britain at the Grand Hotel, Bristol, where Harry mixed with the Duke of Beaufort, television stars such as Jimmy Edwards and Liz Fraser, and music stars such as Acker Bilk.

Being the chairman of the local football club as well as a captain of industry meant he was always in great demand as he could be called upon to enlist the support of some football stars to help boost and publicise a good cause, provide a special moment for a sick child or provide a prize for a raffle or fund-raising cause. Whenever he could Harry Dolman supported good causes, especially if they had their roots in Bristol or the sports he loved.

To show his support for local south Bristol lads, Harry went to Bedminster Down Boys Club when new premises in Winford Grove were opened by the Duke of Beaufort on September 21, 1964.

Said Marina Dolman: "Harry was fiercely competitive and loved sports of all types. He never liked to lose. If he made a bet, even if it was for a small amount, he always wanted to collect his winnings. If you played any game against him he would do everything he could to make sure he was the winner. He wasn't a bad loser - he just preferred to win if he possibly could!"

Of course in 1966 England was the centre of world football. The World Cup Final was played at Wembley and the excitement of the competition, which saw the greatest players on the planet gathering in England, swept the nation. Harry and Marina attended the final at Wembley as guests of the Bristol Rovers directors and their wives.

Of course with England beating West Germany in the final, football fever was at its height and there was huge interest in European teams for the first time.

Harry wanted Ashton Gate to be regarded as a venue for international football but the ground was just not good enough. However, in November 1966 he contrived to bring European football to the ground with a game against Hanover 96 for the Friendship Cup. It all stemmed from Bristol's twinning links with Hanover that had started in 1947, following the bombing of both cities during the Second World War.

Harry told of the links in his programme notes for the game:

"In 1947 when the city of Hanover lay in ruins, its inhabitants suffering from shortage of food and clothing and many of them living in one-roomed shacks amongst the debris, the late Alderman Robert St. John Reade organised a goodwill mission from Bristol.

"Such human sympathy impressed the people of Hanover very much indeed and since that time a close friendship has grown between our two great cities. Working committees have been formed in both cities to foster this link and many exchange visits are arranged each year between schools, youth groups and churches etc. In 1965 for the first time a successful families exchange was organised when a number of Bristol families visited Hanover and in July of this year 12 Hanover families visited Bristol.

"Civic parties from the two cities visit each other during alternate years and when my wife and I were kindly invited at our own expense to join the Lord Mayor's party to Hanover in May of this year, Mr Cooper, editor of the Bristol Evening Post, suggested that it would be a good idea for Bristol City to play an annual match against Hanover 96."

Marina Dolman's German language skills came into use as Harry and Marina met with the chairman of the Hanover team and made all the arrangements for the game in Bristol in the November and a visit to Hanover the following year.

Hanover 96 were in the German Super League at the time playing top sides such as Eintracht Frankfurt and Borussia Dortmund.

One thing that particularly impressed Harry Dolman during the five day visit to Hanover to fix up the games was how the Lower Saxony Stadium (Niedersachsen Stadium) where Hanover 96 played had a capacity of 80,000 and had been built following the Second World War.

The game in Bristol was played out in front of 4,599 fans and it was a big day for one young Bristol lad called Chris Garland, who at 16 had been making a bit of a name for himself in the youth team. Harry Dolman spoke to Fred Ford in the days leading up to the game and it was agreed that Garland would make his debut in the friendly.

John Atyeo had hung up his boots at the end of the previous season and had seen the World Cup paraded in his testimonial game against Leeds United in front of 16,000 fans, but he wrote a programme column saying how exciting it was to see an overseas team with fresh style and players.

City lost the game 3-2 with Marina Dolman presenting the trophy to the winning captain from Hanover.

City finished in 15th position in the table that year and Fred Ford's "job for life" only lasted until September 1967. The team saw a poor start to the season, gaining just three points in the first eight league matches and were thrashed 5-0 by Everton to go out of the League Cup.

Football is a results game and with the team bottom of the table after a 4-2 defeat at home to Blackpool, Harry Dolman acted and sacked the man who had taken Bristol City up just a few seasons before.

He wrote about those events:

"It was a very unpopular decision when we sacked Fred Ford, particularly with the press and journalists. The local paper published hundreds of letters – most of them criticising the board, but despite all this I am convinced we were right in seeking a new manager.

"Fred was a wonderful chap but he was afraid to spend money. The press said we should have put a manager over him, making Fred 2nd in command. I am sure this would not have been satisfactory. New managers like to appoint their own staff.

"One director only was against sacking Fred. He had made such a friend of Fred, going everywhere with him, always agreeing with everything he did and so on. When it came to voting on the matter, he hadn't the courage to vote to sack him. I was very fond of Fred Ford and did everything I could to make him happy with the City, but the club's future was dominant in my mind and first division football was the target. Risks with finance had to be taken and so Fred had to go. The press did not forgive us for a long time.

"Having got rid of Fred Ford we had to find a new manager. It was suggested that I should approach Bert Head, Alex Stock, Frank O'Farrell and a few others. Some were difficult to get hold of, but I contacted everyone without any success. I even asked Bert Tann if he was interested.

"At an evening match about this time, Jimmy Hill – who had been managing Coventry City – turned up. He had been highly successful at Coventry and I took the opportunity of getting his opinion.

"I explained that we wanted a young man with some experience. Almost without hesitation he recommended Alan Dicks, who had been his assistant for three or four years and was still at Coventry

City. Jimmy had left to join the BBC. I remember his words. He said, "He is very keen and dedicated to the game, knowledgeable, but a bit green. He won't let you down if you back him, but ask Derrick Robbins' permission to approach him".

"Derrick Robbins was the chairman of Coventry City and had been a great friend of mine for many years.

"I rang the Coventry City chairman to find out if they would allow us to approach him and at the same time I asked him why they weren't appointing him in Jimmy's place. He said, "Oh, he's not good enough for Coventry" so I was a bit hesitant about proceeding.

"Then I saw Jimmy Hill again and told him of my enquiries about Dicks. He said, "Yes, he's a bit green, but he has got drive, he is ambitious and I think he will do well with a little help from you." I then took the matter to the board and told them all I knew and it was agreed that we should ask him to come down for an interview. I must say we were all very surprised at his personality and happy smile and the honest way he answered our questions won him the job. Every member of the City board was impressed and he was appointed manager of Bristol City that evening.

"When I rang Coventry I was told by Derrick Robbins: "Yes, you can have him. We may not have him as assistant manager, that depends on the new man we appoint".

"The appointment of Alan Dicks was not received by the press very well and a few sarcastic remarks were aimed at me, particularly because he was young and green. My only criticism of Alan is that he was too defensive. I realised the negative reaction to his appointment would make his task harder so I went to intensive measures to make him happy.

"I always insisted that the manager should have a written contract and his first contract was for three years. We found him a house and for the next few years I worked hard to make him happy. I invited him to many functions taking place at my company. He joined me for lunch very frequently and always attended every function at my house. We got along very well indeed. Marina, my wife, also did her best to make Alan and his family happy in Bristol and I think we succeeded. We also organised parties for the players. Of course we did the same when the previous manager was appointed. I looked upon this as part of my job."

Between Fred Ford's departure and the appointment of Alan Dicks there were a few games to negotiate and once again Harry Dolman sat down with Les Bardsley and selected the team. Young Chris Garland, who had been talked about as a great prospect, had only been given one league start by Fred Ford following the Hanover game the year before - and Fred had not even watched the game as he had gone scouting elsewhere.

Harry Dolman insisted the 18-year-old should be given a chance as it would be a boost for the fans and a much-changed line-up, including Garland, faced Millwall at The Den and came away with a creditable draw. There were reports that Harry Dolman was positively "beaming" on the coach on the way back.

Bardsley and Dolman picked Garland again for the next match at home to Hull City and he scored in a 3-3 draw to impress the crowd, who liked to have a new local young prospect succeeding. Harry Dolman was immensely proud of the way the changes to the team had paid off and would always tell people: "I never interfered with team selection. I only ever helped choose the team when we were without a manager. But I did give Chris Garland his debut!"

Harry was now working 10am to 4pm at Brecknells as well as dealing with all the differing opinions on his football club chairmanship and doing a great deal of voluntary and charity work when called upon. Now in his sixties he was determined to spend time with his new wife and they took holidays abroad to ensure Harry got the breaks he needed from the high-powered decision-making life.

But just because he was away on a holiday did not stop Harry from coming up with inventions. Always a keen gambler Harry took Marina to the casinos in the South of France and while there had an idea for a coin-operated roulette machine.

He took the drawing back to Brecknells and a team worked on the machine, designing it so that punters could bet on the spin of the wheel. A prototype was put together and Harry persuaded the management at Ashton Court Country Club to install it for trial use by members of the club. Staff from Brecknells went to the club and tested it by feeding coins into it.

Marina recalled: "Harry loved roulette and he played it in the South of France. He worked on the machine and thought it would be a good idea to put into the hotels, as he often complained there was little to do in some hotels particularly in Barbados.

"It would be a revenue earner for the hotels and something to entertain guests. It went through its tests successfully but the legal position was difficult on how it could be used. We went to Reno and met Harry's agent in America - who was richer than he was.

"We went to Harrah's casino hotel where the owners were very interested in it. Harry was very amused that he was taken to the top floor and found the owners had their own armed guards. Some years later someone came to Harry and bought the rights for the machine for America."

By the end of the 1960s Harry Dolman's expertise in mechanical engineering was being challenged by new electronic devices. The old mechanisms could now be replicated by electronics and he realised that unless Brecknells learned to incorporate electronics into its machines it would be left behind. All this circuitry and electric work was not something that a man in his sixties wanted to learn to do himself so Harry Dolman started looking around for successful firms that were already in that business.

He found a company called Redcliffe Radio, a smaller business than his with around 130 employees, conveniently in Bristol and which was already engaged in producing electronic equipment. In 1965 Brecknell, Dolman and Rogers acquired 51% of the shares of Redcliffe Radio and turned it into Brecknell-Redcliffe Electronics Limited.

Electronics needed to be incorporated into packing, vending and ticket machines and the acquisition proved to be a shrewd move in continuing the success of Brecknells as its team moved into the new generation of machinery.

The move did not go unnoticed. The Queen's Award to Industry was instituted in 1966 for industrial efficiency reflected in increased exports or technological innovation. Harry had always wanted a knighthood, but the next best thing was for the business he had built up and supported for so many years to be recognised by the Queen.

In the awards in 1968 Brecknell, Dolman and Rogers was named as one of the firms to gain this honour.

HRH the Duke of Edinburgh said in a letter to the recipients: "New ideas, new techniques and new materials are being developed more rapidly than at any time in man's history, but there is nothing simple or straightforward in the business of bringing them into economic service. After all the original work has been done, it still depends upon the enterprise and judgement of industrial managements to convert ideas into profitable hardware. If scientists and inventors are honoured for their discoveries then it is only right that manufacturers should be recognised for their part in putting science to practical use.

"It might well be argued that profits are ample reward for

commercial and industrial achievements, but success in world markets also means that the goods and services offered are competitive in price and performance; and competition is the spur of improvement.

"Company profits may vary for any number of reasons beyond the control of the people on the shop floor, but the success of innovations and the improvement of productivity, which alone makes competition in world markets possible, ultimately depends upon their skill and intelligence.

"The Queen's Awards are designed to recognise and to honour all the people who have shown conspicuous success in bringing the fruits of science and technology to the services of man."

Brecknell, Dolman and Rogers was one of 85 firms to be given the honour on the Queen's Birthday in 1968 and the citation specifically mentions how the business had grown four-fold since 1939 and was exporting to 70 different countries.

After listing the huge range of machines being produced by the firm it addresses the latest moves that Harry Dolman had instigated saying: "These machines have been progressively improved and speeds increased until the latest models work four times as fast as the originals. Electronics, manufactured by a subsidiary, Brecknell-Redcliffe Electronics Ltd, are steadily being introduced to improve speeds and reliability."

More than half the packaging and Polymark machines were being exported, bringing wealth into Britain and into Bristol.

The annual report and accounts for the business for the year ended September 1968 showed that the firm was providing work for 1,567 people and that the gross remuneration paid in wages was £1,340,931. Harry Dolman was leading an eight-strong board of directors who had achieved a trading profit of £436,474 on a turnover of just over £3 million.

In his Chairman's Statement Harry Dolman tells how the egg grading and packing machines had been developed with electronic weighing units, which had led to a major award at the International Poultry Show in London and a large volume of orders.

New electronically controlled ticketing machines had also been installed on the Victorian Line Underground in London and more developments were predicted.

He also said: "We have now decided to enter the market for hot and cold drink vending machines and are on the point of concluding an agreement with a well-known American company to manufacture their machines under licence for this country and for Europe. Their machines are claimed to be the best of their kind and have already been sold in large numbers in England."

Another major change was also on the horizon. Britain was to turn to decimal currency and this meant that a huge number of coin machines needed to be converted to enable them to use the new coinage. It seemed certain that Brecknell, Dolman and Rogers, with its expertise, would play a major part in that.

THE DOLMAN STAND

Sitting in the Director's Box every week, looking across the pitch at the run-down facilities opposite him at Ashton Gate, got Harry Dolman thinking. His philosophy that it was not just a team that made a successful football club, but that the facilities were equally important in providing a solid income, was not universally popular with fans or even fellow members of his board.

The stand, rebuilt quickly after the war, housing the dressing rooms, offices and all other facilities, provided uncomfortable seating on wooden slatted seats with a standing enclosure in front of it. To Harry's left from the Director's Box was the Open End, simply stepped terracing where hardy souls stood in the winter and endured all the elements could throw at them during a game. To the right was the Covered End - nicknamed the East End by fans post war - which at least provided some cover. There was nothing that resembled any kind of modern stadia.

While Fred Ford was manager Harry had started to work out how more seating could be provided along the far side of the ground. The musings turned into a legacy that bears his name to this day. He had a "blueprint" which he kept in his safe and which he constantly revisited, trying to work out how the major ground improvement could be achieved. His first discovery was that his plans were restricted by the space available as the club did not own a strip of land on that side of the ground. He told of the early moves:

"Years before the new stand was built I knew that some day it would be done, although there was no enthusiasm for it by my colleagues. They were frightened of the cost. Gilbert Young was my only supporter.

By the time the old shed was condemned and pulled down, our gates were poor and we were still struggling in the 3rd Division, so I began to prepare the ground and work on it quietly alone.

"We did not own the entrance to the ground on that side and there was insufficient room to build a stand the size I envisaged. Fortunately, there was a strip of land about 15 ft. wide running practically the whole length of the pitch and behind the old stand. I found out that this belonged to the Imperial Tobacco Co; so also did the entrance to the ground. I had for years been doing business with that company so I knew several important people there.

"I did not mention the matter to the Bristol City board for fear they might turn it down. After several weeks of negotiation, Imperial Tobacco agreed to give us the entrance to the strip of land in return for two adverts which were to be put up somewhere of their choice. An agreement was drawn up and it was only then that I reported the matter to the board to which, of course, they readily agreed. I remember one director saying of the adverts: "Something else to keep clean".

"We had, in fact, received a lot of complaints about the weeds in this strip of land from our neighbours. That was the first hurdle overcome."

It was a vital move, that ensured there was enough room for the stand and to enable exits and entrances to be created and a walkway behind the stand, which again were vital for it to get licensed for safe evacuation in an emergency.

With south Bristol at the centre of the tobacco industry at that time the smell of tobacco smoke hung thickly in the air every game and the large advertisements for the locally-produced cigarette brands seemed to make absolute sense for everyone - but few realised that without those two advertisements the Dolman Stand could never have been built and the modern Ashton Gate stadium of today would not have been able to have been developed.

As well as providing a good view of matches Harry Dolman was determined that the new stand would be a revenue-earner for the club. There was never much money to go around and most fans preferred for every penny to be spent on players, but by creating a stand that could bring income Harry Dolman was thinking in the long term - more income would mean more money to spend on players that hopefully could bring the success he so desired - taking the club into the top flight.

Harry's blueprint had the answer as to what could be done to make the new stand generate income. He said:

"Those people who can remember that side of the ground at the time will recall what a mess it was in. Very few spectators could view a game from that side; the toilets were in a shocking state and the galvanised iron hoarding had rusted away and hundreds of people got into the ground free.

"I then started the ball rolling for building the new stand. I had been wondering how we could make use of the stand seven days a week instead of about once a fortnight. Indoor bowling was becoming very popular all over England so I made up my mind that bowling rinks should be incorporated.

"In fact, I decided on this before I had obtained the strip of land from the Imperial. I got one of my draughtsmen at Brecknell, Dolman and Rogers to make a layout. The intention then was to have four rinks on the ground floor and two rinks above, but when we obtained the extra space and the matter was in the hands of our architect, he quite rightly arranged six rinks on the ground floor.

"I had always envisaged the rinks being used 12 months of the year by arranging a league competition during the summer which would have meant club teams playing one match a week, but this never came to anything. I found the bowling fraternity a little difficult to deal with. They had set ideas about winter and summer bowling.

"I still think a grand league competition could have been arranged. My idea was to give a prize of something like £100 to the club winning the league. I'm sure a sponsor would have come along to back this and the rinks would have been used 12 months a year. Unfortunately, the directors of Bristol City were not very keen or interested and the new members who came on the board later were almost prejudiced. However, having made the plans for a stand on that side of the ground, I had to find the money to build it. I thought if we don't do it now it will never be done."

Harry was a keen bowler himself and had installed a bowling green in his garden where he hosted matches, including many with Bristol City players, famous footballers from other clubs and an annual Bristol City versus Bristol Rovers fixture.

He was quite right in his assertion that indoor bowls was about to take off in a big way. Soon it would be a televised sport with famous players, such as England's legendary David Bryant, from just down the road in Clevedon, Scotland's John Watson and Wales' Terry Sullivan becoming household names, prompting many people to take up the sport and want to emulate their television heroes.

Harry met up with Peter Brimble, a well-known international bowler in Bristol, who was also an England selector and a leading light in the indoor game. Indoor Bowls was, of course, primarily a winter sport, that allowed those who enjoyed the game in the summer to play it all through the winter months.

Bristol had formed an indoor bowls club in 1948 and there were no purpose-built rinks when the two men talked. The nearest indoor bowls to Ashton Gate was played at Bristol South Baths in

Bedminster. There the swimming pool was boarded over in the winter and a number of sports took place on the boards, including roller skating, boxing, table tennis and gymnastics.

Green baize was rolled out on Mondays and Tuesdays with chalk lines to mark the "ditch" and three rinks created with Bristol City Council collecting the "green fees" from the players. The sport grew in popularity with hundreds of players.

Harry was playing for Bristol St Andrew's Bowling Club and he had followed the saga of Bristol Indoor Bowls Club, who had been trying to build a purpose-built indoor bowling centre at Bower Ashton without success.

Peter Brimble had successfully found the land, got backers and seemed set to make the venue a reality in 1965 but a series of planning wrangles with Bristol City Council led to the project floundering.

When Harry Dolman and Peter Brimble met both men found a solution to their problem - Brimble could get the purpose-built indoor bowls facility he desired and Dolman could get the new 5,000 seats for the football club, with an income generating activity going on beneath it. Peter Brimble's persistence and insistence that membership and revenue would grow convinced Harry Dolman, although introducing another sport into Ashton Gate was never particularly popular with the board or with fans of the football club.

At a board meeting in March 1967 Harry Dolman revealed his blueprint to the rest of the board, who gave it their approval and the rather optimistic headline "£50,000 stand for 5,000 by 1968" appeared in the Bristol Evening Post.

The headline was optimistic in both costs and the speed with which the project might be completed. At that time the talks about the bowling facilities had not been finalised and the public was told that the development of buildings and offices under the stand would have to wait until the money came in. There were also plans to put a small gymnasium under the stand for the players.

The newspaper reported: "Mr Dolman envisages the new stand seats being sold at moderate prices - probably around the 7s. 6d. to 8s. 6d. mark - compared to 12s for the current stand seats. Season tickets would also be considerably lower than the £10 10s at present."

Harry Dolman is quoted as telling the reporter: "We hope to have many of these seats filled by new season ticket holders before the actual building work begins." When asked if the expenditure on the ground meant there was less money for players, he replied: "I think the development of the ground to First Division standard and the improvement of the team go together."

The old stand had been condemned and dismantled reducing the club's seating capacity by a quarter.

Harry had firm ideas about the construction of the new stand and had produced many sketches and drawings himself, some of them on the back of cigarette packets, which were then passed to draughtsmen at Brecknells in Pennywell Road to turn into a workable drawing.

But it was not just the design that was worked out on the back of a cigarette packet - the whole finances of the project came about that way, as Harry Dolman wrote:

"I'd like to tell you a little story about the building of the Dolman Stand. I had been in touch with two businesses, one of which said I could have £65,000 at 2.5%. I put this down on the back of a cigarette packet, added a few other figures and decided we would build the stand. I used to smoke a great deal in those days, something like 50 cigarettes a day, so I had plenty of packets to write on. Some of them were thrown away, sometimes with notes on, otherwise we might have had a double decker.

"When the project was about to be proceeded with, there were those people who said we must have a team before this stand. Others wanted a double decker. What most people don't understand is that it is possible to get substantial sums of money for a project like the stand, but few people are willing to put money into a club to buy players."

Of course a lot of the differences of opinion that Harry talks about were played out in the local newspaper. Not everyone approved of the ideas Harry had worked out on the back of a cigarette packet and a gentleman called T. Hodgson, of Westbury-on-Trym, sent a letter to the Green 'Un sports newspaper in July 1967 with his own views, starting by praising the fact that the new stand was likely to provide wider seats and more leg room than the stand on the opposite side of the pitch, saying: "Anyone sufficiently well fed to be able to afford the price of a seat in the present stand finds some difficulty in squeezing into the space available.

"But, without sight of the sketch plans, one is left wondering exactly what sort of a stand it is going to be. The present stand was hastily conceived in a period of extreme shortages of building materials.

"Those days have passed and there is no real reason why the new stand should not be a thing of architectural beauty as well as comfort, which means a double decker of cantilever construction offering a clear and uninterrupted view of the entire field of play from each and every seat in the stand.

"These are standards that are demanded in all other forms of public entertainment, and which football must provide, and offer at a reasonable price, if it is to survive and prosper. The aim at Ashton Gate should be a seat for every spectator, but that will take time. Meanwhile no provision should be made for standing spectators on that side of the ground to be graced by the new stand. The front row of the existing stand is some 30 yards away from the touchline. That is a waste of accommodation, for the terracing in the enclosure is inadequate for the purpose intended and few of the spectators at a well-attended match get a reasonable view of the game.

The alignment of the seat rows should be elliptical and not parallel with the touchline like the existing stand.

"A double-deck stand worthy of the occasion would be large enough to hold 8,000 spectators and would probably cost about £200,000 instead of the £50,000 mentioned. But at the higher figure it could be an economical proposition at 8s. a seat if the quality of the football is good enough to attract 75 per cent support. It is now or never so let us not miss the opportunity to make Ashton Gate a football ground to be proud of."

Harry found the questioning of his plans annoying and hit back with his own article in the newspaper complete with a sketch that showed that an elliptical stand did not provide better views and would prevent a rear walkway from being constructed behind the stand. He also said that if people were seated in the front row next to the pitch they would not be protected from the elements as the roof could not be extended out far enough.

Everyone had an opinion and when the plans for the bowling greens were announced some fans questioned whether Harry Dolman was now more of a bowls fan than a Bristol City fan and was he trying to make Ashton Gate a bowls venue. He hit back through the media saying: "Remarks that we have sacrificed football for bowling are rubbish - the two are entirely separate, but at the same time are complementary to each other. The main point about the whole project is that instead of having a stand which is going to be used once a fortnight eight months of the year, we shall have one that will be used every day 12 months of the year."

More opinions poured into the media and one letter signed

simply "Supporters and Citizens of Bristol" criticised the fact that Harry Dolman was coming up with the design himself. The letter, published in August 1967, said that names and addresses had been supplied but not published in the local paper "because of a professional reason". It suggested co-operating with the city council so that the land behind the proposed Dolman Stand could become part of the development of the new stand with outdoor bowling greens and community uses.

The letter stated: "At a time when the game is struggling to attract more people to its stadiums it seems that those running its affairs almost always overlook the importance of creating a pleasing and comfortable environment. This is a great pity because football stands present the professional designer with an opportunity to produce stimulating and exciting surroundings yet the result of what is usually produced on our grounds is nothing more than a visual slum."

Tough words and as the letter went on it got more personal about the involvement of Harry Dolman in the design, saying: "What is required is not more money but more imagination and design skill. With these faculties employed to the full, using the money available it should certainly be possible to do as well as Manchester United and Coventry and even better in our view.

"We would be the first to acknowledge Mr Dolman's magnificent efforts on behalf of the club and we feel sure that he would, in turn, acknowledge that professional skills ought to be appropriately deployed in their rightful spheres on the field, in board room and management, and in the creation of exciting structures and environment. We have seen no reference to a specialist in the latter field having been involved in the team and this seems to be an unfortunate omission, which reduces the chances of beating Manchester United!"

Undaunted, Harry Dolman produced a scale model he built himself for the city council planning committee and for fire and police officials. But he told the local newspaper that he had an architect working on the design of the rear of the stand. He said: "We have an architect working on it now because we want the design to be pleasing to the eye, particularly for the people looking out from the flats on that side of the ground."

In August 1967 it was revealed that the estimated cost had now soared from £50,000 to £90,000, and with poor results on the field fans were starting to question whether Harry was putting the club in danger of relegation. It all played in to the sacking of Fred Ford and the appointment of Alan Dicks.

By January 1968 the estimated cost of the stand was now said to be between £130,000 and £140,000 after it was shown that the soft nature of the ground at Ashton Gate meant that between 60 and 80 supports would need to be pile-driven into the ground to support the stand and that, along with the tons of concrete required, would cost at least £25,000.

With a young, inexperienced manager in charge of team affairs building a squad of players whose results were not spectacular, criticism grew from the fans, who started calling for board members to resign. Harry set about working on raising the funds, which he privately already believed would be far in excess of the £130,000 told to the press and fans.

Over the next few months he looked at gaining corporate support, selling some of the club's assets and predicting income as the cost estimates seemed to rise week by week. At times it looked like the stand he had dreamed of building for Bristol City would never come to fruition. He said of those days:

"I wrote to all the large firms in Bristol asking for financial help and

collected about £200. That's how interested the Bristol companies were!

"We had received a quotation of £170,000, which because of complications and delays, eventually rose to £215,000. I was a bit worried to say the least and my colleagues on the board were all in favour of shelving the matter, except for one director, Gilbert Young. He was in 100% favour. Bristol City had no money and they had an overdraft and the bank manager had little sympathy, so it became my job to sort it out.

"The 51 Club was against it and a group from there openly asked the board to resign en bloc. They offered to take over the club and were prepared to make a loan of £30,000 – chicken feed in my estimation. One condition was that the stand project must be dropped.

"We had in fact gone too far with the plans to retract. We had already committed the club to clearing the site, ordering the steel and other work. I was now determined to go through with the project. I knew if we didn't do it now it would never be done. I made an assessment as to how we could get the money:

I asked the directors to put in £3,000 each.	£24,000
We could sell the houses owned.	£45,000
A transfer fee for Stacey.	£ 7,000
Advanced ticket sales for the stand when built.	£30,000
All money from supporters' club.	£10,000
Car park letting in advance.	£ 5,000
Share capital of club to be doubled.	£15,000
New adverts paid in advance.	£10,000
Watneys £65,000 loan at 2.5% interest	£65,000
Free loan from Friend	£ 6,000
	£217,000

Harry's new "back of a cigarette packet" calculation showed how more than £200,000 could be raised; but it meant selling off houses behind the Open End which were owned by the club. Many of them had players living in them and they were not pleased to be thrown out - although Harry Dolman felt that the letting of the houses to players and staff had always been a "fearful burden" to the club.

Marina Dolman said: "He was most disappointed at getting just £200 from local businesses. Everywhere he went he heard the same thing from firms: "If we give you any money then we would have to give the same amount to Bristol Rovers and we can't afford twice the amount". One of the local businesses he went to was Courage brewery and he offered them the chance to be the only beer supplier in the new stand, but they said they couldn't be associated with just one of Bristol's football clubs, so he went to Watney Mann and they were delighted to do the deal which involved them providing a loan at 2.5%.

"In return the club was restricted to only having their beers, wines and spirits for the next 10 years, which didn't please some people further down the line, but did mean the stand was financed.

"There were many critics and many people against the idea of the new stand or some aspect of it but Harry worked hard on getting the finance. There were others in favour - one person came up and gave him £2,000 in cash towards the stand. Harry always thought that the stadium and the players should grow together but they were difficult times."

In April 1968 Harry told the Evening Post reporter Peter Godsiff that the stand was to go ahead, while also revealing expected costs had risen to £140,000 - a rise of £10,000 in three months.

Harry told the newspaper: "Although I was always confident we would not be relegated, we decided to wait until we were absolutely safe before going ahead with the stand. We hope to start the work in the summer but it will not be ready in time for next season."

In the same interview Harry Dolman said he would have resigned as chairman if the club had been relegated to the Third Division; with just three clubs below them it had been a close call. The criticism that he was starving the team of money by persevering with the ground improvements had hit him hard and even though he spoke of money being available for players fans were quick to criticise that they weren't of the calibre needed.

That summer ES & A Robinson (Holdings) Ltd were appointed as architects to modify the original structure that Harry Dolman had designed and the changes they were able to make showed that the criticism through the media from Mr Hodgson and others had an effect and Harry Dolman had taken on board many suggestions.

He told the Evening Post: "The main difference is in the arrangement of the six indoor bowls rinks which form an important part of the structure. Originally four rinks were to be on the ground floor and two on the first floor. As the width of the stand has been increased, all six are now situated on the ground floor.

"By so doing the stand has been made bigger, there will be increased seating capacity to more than 5,000 and it will be a better proposition all round at similar cost. It is not a cantilever stand but I have insisted all along that there should be no pillars to obstruct anyone's view. This has now been successfully accomplished."

The final design of the stand saw a structure 320 feet long, 70 feet deep and rising to a height of 67 feet, towering over the existing roofs at Ashton Gate. A tubular lattice spine girder approximately 15 feet deep was designed to span the entire length of the stand supported by two end pillars - effectively giving a view of the pitch with no pillars. The girder was reported to be the third longest of its kind in the country at the time.

Harry Dolman said proudly, as the architects revealed the model for the new stand with their modifications: "The stand should be as good, if not better, than any stand ever built. I am sure there will be no stand in the country more remunerative than this one. I look upon this as a money-making concern. The popularity of indoor bowls and the lack of facilities in Bristol should make Ashton Gate the bowls centre of the city and the surrounding areas. The bowling authorities are as anxious as we are to see the stand finished."

Peter Godsiff at The Evening Post said: "At the moment the idea is to give a permanent name to the stand. The most popular suggestion so far is "The Dolman Stand" and I have little doubt that the city directors will decide on this name."

By October 1968 the expected cost of the Dolman Stand had soared to £170,000. The club had announced a scheme where supporters could book seats in the new stand but the team was languishing around 17th and 18th in the division leading to some people questioning once again whether players should be bought instead of new facilities. Then there was the matter of getting planning permission through the city council's planning committee.

The plans were submitted and a petition of protest signed by 54 people was submitted to the planners, most of them residents of Southbow House in Duckmoor Road, situated behind the proposed new stand.

Jim Webber, local government reporter at the Post, reported: "The petitioners said it was corporation policy to house elderly people on the lower floors of tall blocks and, inevitably, these residents spent much time just sitting and looking out of their windows. If the proposal went through they would be faced with 'an ugly grey concrete curtain wall."

Talks were held between the corporation and the club and some changes were made. Approval was sought from the Chief Constable and Fire Officer. The issue of car parking was brought up but the plans were finally approved in November with just two councillors voting against it - one because of the view from the Duckmoor Road flats and one because of car parking.

Other councillors argued that the stand would not increase the number of people attending matches, only an improvement in the standard of football on offer would do that!

The standard of football was causing concern and just days after the approval was given the local media was declaring that Bristol City was in "crisis" and that the situation was getting "desperate". City were languishing perilously close to the foot of the table and all this talk of a stand led to fans writing to the newspapers with their own theories of what was wrong.

Alan Dicks had chosen Tony Collins as his assistant manager. As most of his duties involved scouting he had continued to live in Rochdale. The fact he had not moved to Bristol was seen by some fans as a lack of commitment to the cause and questions were being asked as to why he was allowed to live so far away.

Harry Dolman stepped out of a three hour board meeting in November to say: "The local press are not helping. They are only incensing the public." Secretary Bert Bush told the waiting sports journalists: "There is nothing to report. It was just a normal board meeting."

Harry Dolman also rounded on the fans saying they weren't helping by getting at the players and ruining their confidence. Letters were pouring into the local media. A 2-1 home win against fellow strugglers Bury calmed the nerves but the team continued to be in the bottom three of the league as fans were split between those supporting the venture and those feeling they would have a nice new stand but be in the league below.

The programme notes for the Aston Villa game in October told of the more positive reactions to the stand saying: "We are hopeful that the final snags can be overcome shortly so that building work can begin.

"We are delighted to report that the interest among our supporters these past four weeks has been most encouraging. To date more than 200 of the 5,000 seats have been booked.

"Some spectators have paid in full for their seats for the first year; others have given us a reasonable deposit and some people have just written to say they would take a seat once they were being allocated.

"These include a block application of 40 seats from the B.A.C. (British Aircraft Corporation). One of our supporters there has been so impressed by the stand that he has sought support from his working colleagues and has started a subscription fund.

"We are indeed grateful to this supporter and the idea certainly commends itself to employees in other factories, businesses or offices where there are groups of supporters of this club."

Prices for season tickets in the new stand were announced at £6 10s (Equivalent to £6.50 at 2017 prices) £7 10s (£7.50) and £8 10s (£8.50) and in the programme for the next home game against Birmingham City, Harry Dolman announced a new incentive, saying that anyone who booked a season ticket for the first season could have their name engraved on the seat.

In fact it was January 1969 before work started on constructing the new stand and the club had still not been able to sell all of the 16 houses it owned. The club had collected in as many deposits as possible but was still struggling financially. An idea to have a regular market in the car park, charging stallholders £4 for two days, was launched as Harry Dolman tried to scrape together the vitally needed finances for the building.

At the end of the season in May, four months later, City had survived once again, finishing 16th in the Second Division, but construction work on the Dolman Stand seemed slow and fans going to the ground to look at the construction started to question whether it was really going to be ready for the start of the 1969/70 season.

Contractors Nott Brodie stopped work altogether after Bristol City Council's Engineer cast doubts on the structural soundness of the design and the council and the chairman of Bristol City locked horns over the project.

Just a year previously, in May 1968, a 22-strorey tower block in Newham, East London, partly collapsed after a gas explosion. It became known as the Ronan Point disaster as four people died and 17 were injured.

The investigation into that disaster had just been completed and new building regulations were about to come in. The council in Bristol wanted to ensure that the Dolman Stand would meet those new regulations, so all works were stopped while checks were carried out.

It was a terrible blow for Harry Dolman who fumed: "We placed the order for this stand - and we want delivery of the goods. We have had delay after delay. Just what is going on? I don't know and frankly as chairman of Bristol City I am thoroughly fed up with the whole position.

"Bristol planning committee has taken an unhelpful position. In Leeds, and other cities where new stands are being built, planning committees have gone out of their way to make sure stands are built in time for the new season."

At the end of that month Harry Dolman told the Bristol Evening Post: "I have had a letter from one of the contractors, which makes it clear to me that February is the earliest we can expect completion.

"We've had nothing but delays from the start of the operation last November. It is obvious to me that it will be at least another month before the present difficulties are sorted out. We had a firm delivery date for the start of next season when we placed the contract in January. It is all so terribly disappointing."

More than that there were now 1,500 people who had already booked season seats in the Dolman Stand and they were given three alternatives: pay some extra and take a seat in the old stand, where there were only less desirable seats left; wait for the new stand to be built and then take their seat on a 12-monthly basis from when it was ready; or have their money back.

Harry Dolman pleaded with fans not to ask for their money back saying: "I hope everyone will take it on the chin like we had to and back us up on this."

It also meant problems for the City of Bristol Indoor Bowling Club, who had been expecting to play some of the summer season at their new purpose-built venue and instead had to go cap-in-hand back to the council asking if they could resume playing at Bristol South Baths.

Costs had now gone over £200,000 and by December 1969 that was £220,000 and the finances were looking trickier than ever. Despite being at home with a throat infection Harry Dolman announced that season tickets would all have to go up by £1 for the new stand for new people buying them - although those who had shown faith and paid in advance got them at the original prices. He also made an appeal for help as funds were now £10,000 short of what was needed, saying: "If 20 big firms gave us £500 each that would do it. We're as close as that."

Finally in the early months of 1970 the stand began to take shape and by the time City and Rovers fans packed into the ground for the annual Gloucestershire Cup match in April it was starting to look impressive.

Days later Harry Dolman stood on the pitch and watched as the 59 ton girder was lifted into position.

Two cranes, one at either end of the ground, lifted the massive 320 feet long girder up in an operation taking 15 minutes to complete and the full scale of the Dolman Stand could be seen for the first time.

More changes were announced. The pitch, which until then had been 117 yards long by 78 and a half yards wide, was made two yards narrower so that a "schoolboy enclosure" could be put in front of the new stand. Harry Dolman was keen to encourage young fans of the future with a cheap ticket allowing the boys to stand on terrace steps.

This announcement angered a number of fans who said it would be the death of wing play by Bristol City and that once again the chairman was putting his stand before the footballing side of the club.

By May 1970 the stand was taking shape and Harry Dolman told everyone he was going to approach Sir Matt Busby for a gala match against Manchester United to open the new stand. He also came up with a cunning way of saving a little money as the finances were tight.

There were 4,300 seats to be bolted into position; the back two rows of the stand were originally slatted wooden seats as it was felt they would not be occupied often. Instead of paying a workforce to put the new seats in position the football apprentices were called in during July to bolt the new seats into place.

By June 1970 the club was confidently predicting the new stand would be open for business in September with the bowling greens ready for use by October. Harry Dolman admitted to the press that at times he was frightened the club would not obtain the money needed to finance it but he was now happy to reveal exactly how those finances looked as the final estimated cost of the project now stood at £220,000.

In June 1970 the finances were:

Money in hand

Watney loan, other loans, Steve Stacey transfer fee	£105,000
Directors loans	£3,000
Advertisements on stand so far	£2,000
Loans	£2,000
Sale of right of way	£5,000
Total:	£140,000

Cash Expected

Sale of club houses	£35,000
Supporters Club donations	£8,000
Advertisements expected	£9,000
51 Club donation	£1,000
Open Market and Bingo	£5,000
Donations promised from others	£4,000
Sale of Dolman Stand seats	£5,000
Total:	£67,000

At this time there was nothing Harry liked better than going to check the progress of the stand on his way into Bristol. Every day it seemed to take on a new shape and form.

Marina Dolman remembers: "Harry had taken on the role of President of Bristol Chamber of Commerce in 1966 and played a strong part in that organisation. In August 1970 I bought him a lovely silk and mohair suit for his birthday. He wore it for the first time going to a big lunch at the Chamber.

"Of course on his way he couldn't resist stopping off at Ashton Gate to see how the stand was progressing and for some reason he decided to climb over the seats to look at something and managed to tear a huge three quarter rip in his trousers. He went into the offices at Ashton Gate and stuck it up with Sellotape and that was how he arrived at this grand luncheon.

"I was really annoyed and had to get a new pair of trousers made for him. But it showed just how enthusiastic he was about getting things done on the stand."

Around that time another row erupted in the media. This time over the plight of disabled fans. A 70-year-old disabled fan called Charles Adams had watched City play from 1947 until 1968 but after that had watched games from the window of his flat in Winterstoke House. He now found the superstructure of the Dolman Stand blocking the way.

He told the media: "I couldn't see the goals at either end but by watching the build-up play and listening to the crowd's reaction I knew when City had scored. I also used to like watching the boys training when Freddie Ford was the manager.

"The enclosure for invalid chairs is out in the open and I'm afraid I couldn't stick it out for 90 minutes on a really cold day. If they made some space for invalid chairs under the cover of this new stand I shall be back over there for every home game."

Other disabled spectators who received free tickets told how they had been parking their blue three-wheeler cars on the space in front of the Dolman Stand and could now not do so because of the building work going on.

In those days, a quarter of a century before the Disability Discrimination Act came into force, the answer from the club secretary Bert Bush was blunt and to the point.

To Mr Adams he said: "There is no chance of any invalid chairs being accommodated in the new stand. The very front row of seats is at least 14 feet off the ground making it impossible to get any chairs up there."

To the 15 people who had opportunities to park their cars, he said: "I'm not at all sure we shall be able to let the handicapped spectators park in front of the Dolman Stand, at least for the time being. We may, of course, find an alternative spot for them on the ground, but it looks as if we shall have to delay giving out our complimentary tickets until work on the Dolman Stand is finished. The people who receive free tickets must either be escorted by someone or come in their invalid car. If a stand or a fence collapsed, these people would be helpless to defend themselves."

The 1970/71 season kicked off with the stand complete enough for some spectators to use it for the first game against Sunderland. Contractors carrying out work on the stand erected special temporary staircases to allow the 2,378 season ticket holders to access the new stand - but they were not sitting in their paid for seats and many had poor views because of the building material and other teething problems.

City's star player Bobby Kellard had been sold to Leicester City for £49,000 and Alan Dicks seemed to think that an unknown 17-year-old Scottish kid called Gerry Gow could replace him. Again fans and the local media made their feelings known.

A comment piece in the Evening Post read: "Our view is that Bristol City must give serious consideration to buying a new player if they make a bad start to the season. The Bobby Kellard transfer to Leicester has left a gap that we hope Gerry Gow will plug. But if he doesn't, after being given a reasonable run, the club must find money from somewhere to bolster the team.

"It has become increasingly obvious that money is in short supply at Ashton Gate. The Dolman Stand project has fully extended the club's finances and it is clear that the £50,000 from the Kellard sale is going into bricks and mortar and not into team strengthening.

"There is no doubt that the stand is going to be a magnificent asset to the club. But should it take priority over the team? This is an important question the directors must now ask themselves.

"For to have the best-appointed ground in the Third Division would be a tragedy for Bristol and the thousands of City supporters who have tolerated the club's Second Division struggle for four seasons. We hope that any misgivings about this season's playing standards at Ashton Gate will be unfounded. There is nothing we would like more than two promotion-challenging teams in Bristol this season.

"But if City fail to get the winning start they urgently require the directors must get the message early enough to remedy the situation. And in our view that would mean making money available to Alan Dicks for at least one new player."

It was comments like this that led Harry Dolman to say about that period of his chairmanship:

> "I made many mistakes – mistakes I would not make again. I tried to please the press, the shareholders, the managers, the directors and the players.
>
> "The press has done football a lot of good, but it has also done the game a lot of harm. They have an advantage over those governing the game. They advocate a policy on procedure and then criticise the people who try to implement it. If it fails, they can always have the last word. I have met journalists who have been an absolute menace to the club. I could not have built up my own business if I had had to tolerate press men like football clubs have to."

Thankfully the team won a seven-goal thriller against Sunderland 4-3 on the opening day of the season, got a creditable draw 1-1 at Charlton and then beat Cardiff 1-0 at home to find themselves third in the table by the end of August and some of the criticism began to subside - the tigerish Gerry Gow in midfield won over the crowds.

But all was not peaceful in the new stand. Some people complained they couldn't see the near touchline so groundsman Mike Lillington was asked to shift the pitch over to improve sight lines. Harry Dolman also made a point of setting out the full finances of the new stand once again in the match-day programme to show that it had been achieved without using any of the Bobby Kellard transfer fee.

The stand, which when it was first discussed was planned at a cost of £50,000, in fact came in nearer to £235,000, but Harry Dolman said at the time of opening that it would have cost 50 per cent more than that in 1970 prices.

There were a final painful few months to negotiate as the finishing touches to the stand took longer than expected and it wasn't until November 2, 1970, that Harry Dolman bowled the first wood on the new indoor bowling green, watched by Peter Brimble and other members of the City and County of Bristol Indoor Bowls Club.

The bowlers weren't entirely happy with the surface. As a final cost-cutting measure Harry Dolman had employed a building contractor to put down the screed base and had bought the cheapest playing surface, thick baize, instead of greengage. But the indoor bowling centre was completed and was bringing in finances for Bristol City.

The next day a force eight gale tore panels off the Ashton Park end of the stand just hours before Bristol City were due to play at home to Leicester City in the League Cup and construction workers had to run for cover.

The match went ahead with a gaping hole in the side of the new stand and some seats out of bounds for safety reasons.

Although the Dolman Stand was not perfect it was the first piece of modern stadium structure to be built at Ashton Gate and it is now incorporated into the modern all-seater stadium. The schoolboy enclosure in front of it was popular for many years before being replaced with seats and the income from the bowls proved to be vital to the football club's survival in the early 1980s when financial problems hit.

Harry Dolman had certainly made his mark on the club, but while he was navigating the twists and turns of making the stand a reality he was also passing retirement age and thinking about how he could step down from Brecknell, Dolman and Rogers.

STEPPING DOWN

A t the end of the 1960s Harry Dolman wanted to spend more time with his wife. He was now over 70-years-old and his business was facing major changes. Decimalisation was on the horizon. This would mean big changes in the vending machine and coin-operated market. New 5p and 10p coins were introduced in 1968 identical to the shilling and two shilling pieces. But the planned new 50p piece, which was to replace the 10 shilling note in October 1969, and other decimal coins coming in for D-Day in February 1971, would not be so easy to accommodate.

Electronics were becoming more and more important and although he had acted to ensure the business had an electronic capability it was still outside Harry Dolman's personal comfort zone as a mechanical engineer. He had worked hard. He had earned his fortune. It certainly seemed time to find someone else to run Brecknell, Dolman and Rogers while he spent more time enjoying his leisure time, holidays and, of course, football.

He wrote of the process he went through in trying to work out what to do to enable the business to carry on and thrive without him:

> "For five years before my retirement I had made up my mind to give up - but how was I to do it without risking a fortune which my family and I had in BDR? I had already decided there was no one at the company capable of taking over. Those people who might have been able were already too old and the younger ones were not up to it in my opinion so I decided to let it be known that BDR was ready for a takeover.

"Several firms were interested and preliminary offers were made none of which matched my ideas so the matter drifted on. I then thought of appointing a new managing director and engaged a firm of consultants to advertise and bring forward a short list of three or four. This had just got to fruition when out of the blue two new firms became interested and to a little degree I played one against the other. After all, my company was a very prosperous concern and the future as far as I could see was very bright indeed. Nobody could therefore blame me for asking a good price. We had a wonderful machine shop, good factories and some very highly skilled men as well as a good order book. There were also five or six new inventions which had had my undivided attention for the past three to four years. They were all almost ready for the market but still required careful nursing."

One of those firms was the Vokes Group, which had its headquarters in Guildford and which had a history dating back to 1920 when it had been founded by C.G.Vokes. The firm's chairman Sir Ian Stewart-Richardson, who had been appointed on public flotation in 1936, was suffering ill health and in the final days of his life. A new forward-looking board saw Brecknell, Dolman and Rogers as a good diversification while staying within the engineering market.

During the Second World War Vokes had produced 3,000 types of air filters for the services and had manufactured parts for the Mosquito aircraft. In the late 1950s they had acquired a firm that made artificial limbs and orthopaedic appliances and had grown the business so that by the time they were in talks with Brecknells they were the largest producer of such products in Europe.

Harry Dolman saw parallels with his own business and saw that, with their engineering background, Vokes Group might develop the machinery from Brecknell, Dolman and Rogers to the next stage, as he stepped aside.

The Vokes Group was essentially a "holding company" with a General Engineering Division, which made up 70 per cent of the group turnover. It manufactured filtration systems, and effluent treatment equipment and other specialised engineering products, including pipe supports and expansion bellows, food and tobacco processing equipment and metal treatment plant. The Orthopaedic Appliances Division made up the other 30 per cent of turnover.

In the offer document sent to shareholders in July 1969 it stated: "BDR's main activities are complementary to the manufacture of food and tobacco processing machinery carried on by Vokes; and the effects of the merger will be to provide diversification into an expanding market and to enable the combined group to offer a wider service to the tobacco, confectionery and food processing industries. It is intended that BDR will maintain its separate identity within the group and continue to operate from its premises in Bristol."

Harry Dolman echoed those views in a letter to shareholders setting out the offer and recommending acceptance.

He said: "Vokes provides an industrial partner whose business to a considerable extent is complementary to that of your company and whose management will be a source of additional strength to that of your board. The food and tobacco processing machinery produced by Vokes, together with the packaging and vending machines produced by BDR, will enable the new group to provide a more complete service to our joint customers and at the same time provide benefits to the new group by the more logical use of research and development teams, sales forces and service maintenance organisations."

With Harry Dolman planning to join the board of Vokes it seemed the perfect solution. The final accounts of Brecknell, Dolman and Rogers before take over showed the highest turnover ever at £2,794,656, excluding the electronics work of Brecknell-Redcliffe.

Harry Dolman said in his final Chairman's Statement: "I hardly need say that our order book at the moment is better than it has ever been and I am confident that 1969 will break records with both turnover and profit."

The impressive figures and Harry's optimistic view of the future, including plans for new drinks vending machines and orders coming in for converting machines for the new currency, meant a deal was concluded. Harry Dolman wrote of the deal:

"Vokes took over the company. I was pleased because they were engineers although in my opinion they had not had experience in the high class engineering field that we had grown up in.

"I promised that so far as I was concerned, personally, there were no strings attached to the take over. I could be their servant as long as they wanted me to be. I was anxious that the company should continue to prosper and all those employed should continue with the good employment which I contended they had had up to that time with Brecknell, Dolman and Rogers.

"My understanding was Vokes promised that the company would go roughly on as before at Pennywell Road and all those employed would continue to be employed. I was also asked if I would stay for a year or 18 months whilst they were taking over. I would have done anything to help the take over. On the other hand I was willing to clear out at their request at short notice. I knew they had a problem on their hands. The company had been run by me for years. I knew the majority of the people working there. I knew the trouble makers, and there were a few, but I knew how to handle them. I also knew where the problems sprang from, the productions that wanted watching most of all and where the break down in production was most likely to occur or where there was likely to be a shortage of work. I watched this very carefully and tried to have another job which I could put into production at once to save redundancy.

"I was continually designing or having designed new ideas to prevent a shortage of work. Years before I swore that once a man was employed by my company he was there for as long as he wanted to be, providing he behaved himself. Many times the production of a certain machine came to an end but I always found something to take their place and the numbers employed by the firm was all the time increasing.

"After over 30 years of being the boss, in August 1969 I suddenly found myself without any authority. We had been taken over.

"The last two years I felt the strain of running the company and during that time I was trying hard to find someone to take my place. I was willing to pay almost anything for the right man; six people had been selected for interview but Vokes came along just at that time and I thought this solved the problem.

"My colleagues on the board were either too old or not up to the job of running the company. I had had a hand in the design and development of everything we made, it came natural to me and I loved it. I was the PRO of the company; I also dealt with the staff and work people's problems. I was the personnel officer.

"I was already six years over retiring age and found the going hard. People said it was showing in my face and advised me to pack it in. This was almost as hard because I loved the job I was doing. However, health had to be considered so I sold out to Vokes with a promise from them that everyone would retain his job and the company would go on practically without change.

"When I handed it over BDR had a wonderful reputation worldwide. We had just made a profit of £430,000. We had the largest sales book ever.

"We were expecting a profit of at least £600,000 for the coming year. We had completed the spade work on a machine for putting butter into small half pound tubs at very high speed. We had completed the development of an entirely new ticket issuing machine for the underground railways. This embodied a counting mechanism of my own design which counted coins of various denominations at very high speed and rejected counterfeits; a large order was in hand.

"We had almost completed the development of an entirely new vending machine. We had done most of the spade work on a new drinks machine, which went into production after I left. We had just developed a new machine for fixing labels to new garments and had started producing these machines.

"The roulette machine was now ready for production as were a number of other developments. All the above projects had been put in hand to fill up any gaps in production which might occur in the future. We had also, of course, all our regular lines all selling well."

In August 1969 Vokes proudly said that the acquisition, which had been on the basis of an exchange of shares, had resulted in an increase of nearly £1 million in the issued share capital of Vokes Group Limited, and Harry Dolman was elected onto the firm's board. Even before acquiring Brecknells the firm had a turnover in excess of £9 million and profits of more than £1 million.

Harry Dolman thought that he had found a safe haven for the business he had put so much of his life into and with a place on the board and an understanding that the business wanted his expertise around he felt he had done the right thing. But the realities of not being in total control did not take long to hit home.

He told the story this way:

"I had been chairman and managing director for about 30 years. In my place as chairman they appointed a gentleman who was about my age who had no experience whatsoever with the type of machines we were producing.

"The managing director appointed was also someone unfamiliar with our type of production. To assist him as joint managing director they appointed a man with very little technical experience, a person incidentally due to retire, so straight away there were no technical brains at the top capable of carrying on the company's highly specialised business and all the people appointed in these important positions were old, not young as they should have been.

"As far as myself was concerned I was asked to stay for 18 months to two years, to which I readily agreed. Within a month of the documents being signed I was asked to leave. This I accepted because I had not had a holiday for some time. I was feeling under the weather so I went off on a combined holiday and sick leave.

"Because of the take over I had had no holidays during that summer and was about ready for a rest. I became redundant. I was told that they could not take over whilst I was there and would I clear out by Christmas.

"I had flu and a holiday, which took up most of the time remaining before my redundancy. I was given a directorship of the Vokes Group and became a consultant for BDR for the next 15 months. Meetings were held and other changes in personnel were made but I was never consulted. I was appalled at some of the changes made.

"At the time of the take over a large contract had been received for converting all big machines to the new money. I had had little to do with this because it was considered to be simple and straight-forward but unfortunately the maintenance department was not consulted and the result was the designers tried to do too much.

"They tried to make the converted machines more up to date than anything we had so far made. They also tried to make some mechanisms suit not only recently produced machines but the very old machines.

"To make things worse a new method of robbing the existing machines had come to light; consequently Vokes went into a flap.

"I was away on my overdue holiday and sick leave when all this came to light. I had on many occasions dealt with such problems and when I returned I offered to deal with this problem. I had studied the matter carefully and had thought up a scheme which would have done the job without undue alteration or redesign and practically all the parts already made could have been used. But Vokes said no, we are going to completely redesign the mechanism on entirely different lines and two people with very little experience on vending machines were instructed to make new designs.

"I begged them to let me deal with the matters in my own way but no, they knew best and they duly produced new designs - one of which was selected. Imagine the cost of scrapping the thousands of parts which had been made and all the jigs and tools and the cost of the new tools and new parts for thousands of machines. When the new design was completed I was asked if I would vet it. The machine was sent out to my home and I reported that it was too complicated. Furthermore the machine they sent out to me could be robbed very easily. This was also reported. I was told they knew all about that and would rectify it but they still refused to allow me to alter the machine in any way and thusly save all the complaints, which had already been made.

"It would have taken about 10 days to alter the machine to my ideas and instead of making a loss a profit would have been made.

"A few weeks later I was asked to attend a meeting at lunch time at the factory. It was usual for the directors to sit together. On this occasion I was pushed away to a separate table and had no contact with people who had for years been my colleagues on the board.

"I felt bitterly disappointed and that was the last time I went inside the factory. During the last few weeks of my employment with the company a director from the Vokes Group came to BDR for about one day a week. He was doing the reorganising. I was never consulted.

"I resigned from Vokes forthwith because of the way my company was being managed. I sent in my resignation and I told them at the next AGM that Director Don Ringe and Chairman Charles Hardie should resign. I could see then that Brecknells was heading for bankruptcy."

Bristol City were playing a friendly at Bordeaux in France and Harry Dolman found himself on a flight from Bristol sitting alongside Bristol Evening Post sports reporter Peter Godsiff. He casually told him during the flight about his resignation and the reporter duly rushed to the telephone once in France to get the news back to the paper.

Far from being the happy hand-over that Harry Dolman expected he had set in train a series of events that was to see the business closed down in Bristol within four years. The events included union rows over the handling of redundancies, accusations and counter accusations over the running of the business and Harry Dolman personally found himself on the wrong end of anger from old friends and work colleagues, being blamed by some for allowing the once proud business to be run down.

Charles Hardie, who Harry Dolman had called on to resign, put a different slant on the troubles involved in the decimal-coinage switch to the one outlined by Harry Dolman, when he penned an annual Chairman's Statement in August 1970.

It said: "Brecknell, Dolman and Rogers Limited, acquired on 1st August, 1969, has been absorbed into the group, but not without some difficult problems. That company, which is a leading manufacturer of automatic vending machines, was actively engaged at the time of its acquisition in the changeover to decimal coinage.

"As referred to in the interim statement of December, 1969, and the further statement last February, certain conversion contracts - relating to cigarette vending machines - ran into trouble which it has only been possible to solve very recently. The financial effect of this has been that it was necessary to provide the sum of £595,000 out of the profits of that company prior to acquisition to cover the estimated costs of design modifications."

He told how this had affected the profitability of the business and said: "The whole episode has been a great disappointment but one which has been vigorously tackled and put right."

In late 1972 the Vokes Group was itself taken over by the Thomas Tilling Group. The Imperial Tobacco Company decided not to use vending machines for its products, which proved another blow for Brecknells.

Tilling management looked at the situation and decided that there was no future for the Bristol operation and on March 2, 1973, issued notices to the trade unions, customers and the press, saying they intended to close the works.

About 500 employees in Bristol and 80 service engineers faced redundancy and old machinery was sold off while newer machinery was transferred to manufacturing facilities in Burnley, Lancashire.

Harry Dolman was so furious he made an appearance at one of the works meetings to speak to some of the former employees. Arguments over the closure rumbled on and in May 1973 Arthur Palmer MP, prompted by union leaders and Brecknell workers in his constituency, raised the matter in the House of Commons in an adjournment debate.

In January 1973 Britain had joined the European Economic Community (EEC) and Arthur Palmer made the point that Brecknells had been cited as just the sort of business that would benefit from the move.

In his description of the firm Arthur Palmer praised Harry Dolman, calling him a "pioneer" and saying the firm had built up a wide reputation at home and abroad for the quality of its products while Harry Dolman was there and that there had never been any suggestion when he was at the helm that the business was anything but successful.

He said how the news of the closure had come as a surprise and the fact that the number being made redundant was said to be 500 when the number of people employed at the time the business was taken over was 1,600 was evidence that it had been "run down".

He also read a letter he had received from Patrick Meaney, managing director, putting the blame for the closure firmly on events before Vokes took over.

Meaney's letter read: "The principal reason for the transition of profits in Mr. Dolman's day to losses in the Vokes era appears to be that, at the time of acquisition, Vokes were not aware of the large and continuing problems of decimal conversion of the vending machine range."

Arthur Palmer retorted: "If that were so, it does not speak very well for the Vokes' accountants that this company was taken over without, apparently, adequate investigation of the future costs that would be incurred by decimalisation adaption."

Tony Benn, MP for Bristol South-East, also spoke up for the workforce and called for a formal inquiry into what had happened. The Under-Secretary of State for Trade and Industry, Mr Anthony Grant, entered the fray, saying: "Vokes took a commercial risk based on the available information, but it was not until it was in charge that it realised that it had not identified many problems which it now believes contained the seeds of the firm's subsequent troubles."

Harry Dolman certainly believed that had he been allowed to work on the decimalisation problems he would have kept the business going.

In the middle of these difficult few years Harry Dolman received an OBE in the New Year's Honours List at the start of 1970 for Services to Export. The national recognition for the work he had done over the years had come at last - not quite the knighthood he had dreamed of but a national honour of which he was proud. But coming, as it did, at a time when he felt frustration at losing control of the business he had spent so many years building up, and with many of the people he knew facing difficult times at Brecknells, it was not something that he felt he could shout about.

Now retired, and not enjoying the best of health, Harry Dolman was also looking at what might be the best future for Bristol City Football Club.

MR BRISTOL CITY

At Ashton Gate manager Alan Dicks was slowly building his team but every year up until the 1971-72 season the club languished in the bottom half of the table. Younger members of the club's board had different ideas to those of Harry Dolman and things were not sweetness and light on or off the pitch.

Before every season Harry Dolman invited the whole squad to his house to play bowls but he was also spending long periods during the season abroad on holiday. During the 1972 season, player Les Wilson was fined £50 after getting into an altercation with Western Daily Press Sports Editor Herbert Gillam, a good friend of Harry Dolman, at a hotel in Carlisle. As a result the press had been banned from travelling with the team, which led to bad relationships with the media.

Financial Director Graham Griffiths predicted a pretty dire situation as the 1973-74 season got under-way and with results not improving there were questions over how long a contract Alan Dicks should be given when it was due for renewal and just how the club was going to get back onto a firm financial footing.

Harry Dolman wanted the directors to all put money in. He also believed that having just a one-year contract might concentrate the manager's mind on getting the best out of the team. Having sold his business and witnessed the problems there he was also looking at who in the Bristol City boardroom might take over. Robert Hobbs, a quarry-owner and self-made millionaire, was on the board and keen to put his own ideas into practice.

In January 1974 Harry Dolman was due to go on holiday to Barbados and he decided to put his ideas to a board meeting before

179

he left. He had been used to the board agreeing to his ideas over the years, but the days of "Harry pulls a leaver and the hands shoot up" had gone. He left the proposals with the other board members to "think about" while he was away.

He described those days:

"For a long time I was thinking of retiring as chairman. I had put it off because I could see no one already on the board who, in my opinion, was capable of taking over. I was hoping someone would come along and join us who would be able to take over. Griffiths and Hobbs had been on the board about one or two years respectively and both had high hopes of taking over. Neither had the right experience and the latter, in my opinion, was much too old. He had – again in my opinion – no or little knowledge of football and less in management of football.

"Griffiths had less knowledge of football and football management, but was supposed to be an expert on figures and for months after his joining the board he was pestering the secretary to get figures out for this and that which, to my mind, was a waste of time. We had never been able to pay our way from gates and were losing money every year on gate receipts. The only thing which saved the club was the odd transfer, a little success in the cup now and again and the money I put into the club, plus the work my firm did for nothing.

"I had been trying for years to raise the income from fund-raising schemes. The supporters club pools and other schemes, the 51 Club, Robins Club, bowls club, and adverts, all helped to keep the club alive. Unfortunately wages and expenses kept rising, so the problem remained the same. There was, in fact, only one way to solve the problem – success on the pitch. It didn't need elaborate figures to tell me this. Running a football club is very different to running any ordinary business.

"When Mr Hobbs came on the board I was told by different people that he intended to alter everything and that changes would be made from top to bottom so, as I saw it, he had made up his mind to become chairman. I was hoping he would be willing to lend the club a sizeable amount of money. I would have willingly stood down for this and in fact would have been willing to make a personal loan of £50,000 interest free.

"In January 1974 we held a board meeting just previous to my going away on holiday. I thought this an appropriate time to discuss the matter with the directors. Unfortunately we were slipping down the table and getting very near to the relegation zone. Bobby Gould had been sold and two players bought with the money, neither of which proved good enough to stop our slide downwards.

"Alan Dicks had been with us about six years. I thought his judgement was a bit doubtful and I did not agree with his defensive style of line up and he was just coming to the end of his contract. I suggested, therefore, that we should not give him, for the time being, another long contract. I thought if he was told that he would only be given a year to year contract until he got success, it would make him realise that more was expected of him. I had spoken to at least four directors on this matter and they all agreed.

"Other proposals I made at this particular board meeting were:

1. Cut the training staff. We were, in my opinion, top heavy.
2. Have a more careful watch on expenses. It was terrible the way money was handed out.
3. I asked for better relations with the press. They had deteriorated badly. There was a ban on the press man travelling with the team. I wanted this ban removed.
4. Some directors were advocating breaking the agreement with the bowling people. I said I would resign immediately if

this happened.

5. There was another suggestion from some directors that we should break the agreement with Watney Mann, who had lent the club £65,000 with an interest rate of only 2.5%. I said I would resign immediately if this agreement was broken.

6. I suggested we should find ways and means of reducing our overdraft. I pointed out that interest rate of about 16% was more than we could carry.

"This meant possibly the directors lending the club money. At the time, each director had a small loan with the club. I was willing to increase mine considerably. I knew I was on a sticky wicket with this suggestion, however, those were my suggestions and I said you can discuss it whilst I am away on holiday and we can then talk it over when I return."

Harry Dolman was away for around three weeks during which the team had a wonderful run in the FA Cup. After beating Hereford United 1-0 away in the Fourth Round they were drawn at home against the mighty Leeds United in the Fifth Round.

It was Don Revie's Leeds United with star names like Bremner, Lorimer, Hunter and Alan Clarke. Cocky and confident, they were the best draw that any lower division club could get at the time. The board decided to put the tickets on sale at the next league match against Cardiff City, which meant a bumper crowd of 24,487, up from just over 11,000 at the previous league game.

A crowd of 37,141 packed into Ashton Gate, bringing receipts of £28,111 to the club, for the visit of Leeds. Billy Bremner scored a screamer of a goal from 25 yards to put the big name stars 1-0 up at half-time but Keith Fear equalised to make it 1-1 on the day and force a replay and another big money day at Elland Road.

It was the time of the three-day week and floodlights were banned to save electricity, so the game against Leeds was played just three days later on the following Tuesday. The club booked the League Liner train - a special train chartered by the football league that season - to take fans to Yorkshire.

Tickets went on sale on Sunday morning and sold out quickly. Some 47,182 packed into Elland Road to see Leeds United take to the field, each player sporting garter tabs with their number on, all gathering in the centre circle to wave at the crowd. The FA Cup draw for the next round had paired the winners against Liverpool. Liverpool manager Bill Shankly told a TV audience: "Leeds versus Liverpool will be the tie of the round". Everyone was expecting Bristol City to have a "nice day out" but ultimately lose out to one of Europe's best teams at the time.

But a stubborn Bristol City side held Leeds in the first half and then, in the 73rd minute, Donnie Gillies scored to pull off the FA Cup shock of the year. His celebrations made the front page of The Times. It was such a big story that it was the first time in its history that The Times had used a sports picture on its front page. Bill Shankly went into the Bristol City dressing room after the game to personally apologise to the players for his remarks before the game and told them they deserved their win.

Even more importantly for a club that was in financial difficulty was the £32,283 in takings, with another big game to come against Liverpool.

Before that game against Leeds Harry Dolman returned from Barbados. He found that his fellow board members had been discussing the views he had put forward before he left. They had interpreted it as something of an "ultimatum" and now, encouraged by the better financial position the club had found itself in, believed it was time for the Dolman era of chairmanship to come to an end.

Harry Dolman told how his time as chairman ended:

"I had only been back in my house a few hours when there was a telephone call to say that Robert Hobbs would like to see me and was coming out straight away. Robert was vice chairman at the time – a new vice chairman was elected each year.

"When he arrived I let him in personally and gave him a drink. He then told me that at a meeting held whilst I was away, it was unanimously agreed to ask me to resign. I was to be offered a life Presidency. I was also promised any tickets I wanted for any match and a free entry to the board room at any time. All this, of course, was offered to me to soften the blow. He added that they could not agree to any of my suggestions and he said they were looked upon by the board as ultimatum.

"I asked who was to become chairman and he replied that he was vice chairman and he would take over the chair for the time being. I said, "You have got what you have wanted at last, but I did not expect to be kicked out whilst I was on holiday." He said, "If you think that, I won't take it".

"I did not want an open conflict with the board. I had plenty of support within the club and outside and many people wanted a showdown, but this was not my idea.

"The extraordinary thing is that all the suggestions I had made were put into effect, except the one referring to the bank overdraft. This went up considerably in the next few months for various reasons including the fact that all directors loans were paid back, which is something I would have opposed.

"They asked me to sell my shares to the board, which I agreed to do. Together with some more in my wife's name and some in my daughter's, we had a total of about 3,500.

"I wasn't happy with the way things had been handled so I thought

I would have a bit of fun with the shares I held. I told them I wanted 24 shillings each for them. I received a letter from Robert Hobbs saying they wouldn't pay over £1 and that they intended issuing another 30,000, i.e. doubling the capital. I knew they would not do this because it meant possibly losing control or having to buy the shares themselves, so I said, "Right, I will give them to my wife and she can sell them to whom she likes".

"They were afraid that these shares would finish in the hands of some opposition, so a few days later I received an offer of 24 shillings each for the lot. The directors had decided to split them up between them.

"I never thought much of the business acumen of some of the directors and this made me think a lot less. That is how my chairmanship came to an end after 25 years. I reckon during the time I was chairman it cost me well over £80,000 including the gift I made to the club in the early 60s."

Harry Dolman took his place in the Directors Box on March 9 when Bill Shankly brought his Liverpool side to Ashton Gate for the FA Cup Sixth Round. But this time it was the top flight club that came out on top in front of 37,671 fans, but it brought a further £28,828 into Bristol City's bank account. The behind the scenes boardroom wrangles had been kept under wraps but just a few days later the news was broken in a statement to the press, who took a photograph of Harry, Marina and their dog called City in the garden of their home.

Harry Dolman's public resignation statement was a masterstroke in getting his digs in at the board members who he felt at that time had been less than grateful for his work. He got in a dig at the manager, encouraging him to attack more, thanked the press (who at the time were still barred from the team bus) and the bowls club (who some of his fellow directors were keen to see leave). All of this while gently pointing out all the work he had done for the club.

The statement read:

"I have to retire some time and now seems to be a grand opportunity - the team has been riding on the crest of a wave, the financial position is good and the league position is much improved.

"We have a good young side and if the manager will adopt a much more vigorous attacking attitude, I believe the team will very soon win promotion.

"The ground facilities are pretty well up to First Division standard and I thank God I had the courage to push through the new stand which the club will find a great asset in the future.

"As chairman during the past 24 years I have seen many ups and downs but have tried never to become disheartened. When I became chairman the ground, the team, the buildings such as they were, were all in a shocking state. I had to face the problems of building the team, improving the pitch, making the ground worthy of English League football and building two stands.

"Football has prevented me from taking at least two trips around the world but I have enjoyed working for Bristol City. It has been hard work but very interesting. In fact I could write a book about it all.

"I am grateful to all those directors who have supported me in the past and wish the present board good luck. I am also grateful to our great Supporters Club, the 51 Club, the Robins Club and the Indoor Bowling Club, all of which I am proud to have established.

"Members of the press too, particularly the local press, I would like to thank for their co-operation over the years. They have always been very helpful to me.

"Finally I would like to express my very great thanks to all those die-hard Bristol City fans and supporters who have loyally attended our matches week after week through the good and bad times.

"Their letters of encouragement and expressions of good faith - particularly during times of stress - have helped me considerably and I shall always be very grateful to them. It is they who make Bristol City the great club it is and I wish them and their club all the luck in the world. I shall continue attending the matches and hope soon to see First Division football at Ashton Gate."

The Evening Post's Peter Godsiff wrote a tribute under the headline: "City will not be the same without Harry". Although the two men had often clashed in their respective roles - Dolman intent on keeping some of the club's affairs confidential; Godsiff charged with the task of informing the Bristol public of as much information as possible about their football club - it was a warm-hearted piece.

Peter said: "I shall always remember Harry James Dolman OBE for his shameless optimism and his fetish for gambling. He was never a defeatist and always believed that City would come out on top no matter the odds against them.

"His gambling, from my personal knowledge, was more to establish principles than to make money. He once struck a bet with me for half-a-crown. He won, demanded his money, and gained as much satisfaction out of that than if he had won the pools.

"Although he made mistakes, everything he did was for the benefit of Bristol City. And he loved talking to the press and getting in the papers - just as reporters loved talking to him.

"He was always helpful to an extreme, courteous, approachable, co-operative. Never did he miss a chance to promote the image of the club.

"I am sorry to see him leave but I believe Robert Hobbs, his successor, can carry on the Dolman traditions. His approach will be different but his ideals will be the same.

"And if City can get promotion during Mr. Dolman's period as the first-ever City president no one will begrudge him the credit for the mammoth part he has played at Ashton Gate since he joined the board in 1939."

When Harry Dolman stood down as chairman of Bristol City the stand that bore his name was a major asset to the club bringing in revenue; the club's overdraft had been pruned to around £100,000 and the squad of players was valued at around £500,000.

Harry set about his new presidential duties with gusto, but gave space to the new board to allow them to do things their own way. He didn't entirely agree with everything they did but he saw that they had the same ambition as himself - to bring top flight football to Ashton Gate - and he did all he could to support that aim, while also taking more time out now he was in his late 70s for travel, holidays and fun.

STANDING OVATION

O ne of the last things that Harry Dolman did before he stood down as chairman at Bristol City was to approve the signing of Paul Cheesley for £30,000 from Norwich City. Cheesley was a local lad from North Somerset but Norwich had been snapping up West Country talent for a while with a good scouting network in the area. At the same time veteran Ernie Hunt signed from Swindon. Both proved to be strong assets to the club.

Manager Alan Dicks was beginning to build a side capable of making it into the top flight - the games against Leeds and Liverpool had given some belief to the young players in the squad and made them realise that they could compete with the best. It also put the club in the national spotlight.

City finished 16th in the table that season and the next year had a reasonable promotion challenge that was only killed off over Easter, leading to a fifth place finish in a league table that was headed by Manchester United, who had dropped out of the top flight and bounced straight back.

The 1975/76 season saw the club competing at the top of the table right from the outset of the season and promotion was on the cards. Harry Dolman was now 78 and suffering some ill health. He went to as many matches as he could but in March 1976 spent two weeks in hospital having an intestinal operation and was unable to go to a game for six weeks.

Tuesday April 20, 1976, is a day etched in Bristol City history. Two points were needed to clinch promotion to the top flight for the first time in 65 years. A crowd of 27,394 packed into Ashton Gate under floodlights. Among them was president of the club Harry

Dolman, determined to see the game despite his recent illness, and taking his seat in the Director's Box.

Clive Whitehead scored the only goal of the game, to beat Portsmouth, sending fans into delirium and Bristol City into the First Division. Harry stood proudly in the Director's Box watching the scenes of mayhem unfold on the pitch as the crowd invaded to celebrate, lifting their heroes onto their shoulders.

Chairman Robert Hobbs had 144 bottles of champagne delivered to the ground to celebrate - and on this occasion Harry Dolman did not object to the players celebrating their great achievement.

Four days later the team played its final game of the season against Notts County and once again Harry Dolman went to the ground to enjoy the party atmosphere. This time, as he went to his seat in the Director's Box, he noticed that spectators in the Grandstand were standing to applaud. He looked around; the fans in the Covered End were also applauding enthusiastically.

Suddenly he realised the applause was for him. Looking over at the Dolman Stand, every spectator was standing and applauding. Harry Dolman received a standing ovation from the whole ground. They had remembered his role in getting the club to this success; the money he had put in; the way he had helped develop the ground and the years of dedication and effort in time and money.

There was a tear in his eye as he waved to the fans in appreciation and took his seat. Of course Bristol City managed to lose 2-1 - so maybe there had been too much champagne and partying, but that's football and little could dampen the enthusiasm at Bristol City - the Robins were going up!

Letters and telegrams of good wishes flooded into Harry Dolman's home from all over the world. Most people had heard of his ill-health and wanted to wish him a speedy recovery while also congratulating him on the role he had taken over the years in keeping the dream of top flight football alive.

Former players, friends, charity workers and even his bank manager wrote to Harry to celebrate with him the success of gaining the First Division status. He was most delighted to receive a letter from his old Commanding Officer in the First World War saying that Bristol City should be grateful that the German soldiers he encountered in the front line while on horseback were not better shots, as it was only because they missed that the club had got to this stage!

Letters were also published in the local papers acknowledging his role as "Mr Bristol City" and saying the achievement would never have happened without him dipping into his own pocket over the years to finance the club.

A few months later Bristol City ran out for their first game in the First Division. The Football League fixture list made it a classic - away to Arsenal at Highbury. The TV cameras were there to see how Malcolm MacDonald, the most expensive transfer of the summer, got on at his new top club. Bristol City, with a team identical to the one that had clinched promotion against Portsmouth a few months earlier, surely had no hope.

Harry Dolman took his seat in the famous Highbury Stadium and watched as Paul Cheesley rose to head in the only goal of the game and pull off a shock 1-0 win to announce their arrival among the big guns.

Even while enjoying being president of a top flight football club, the business acumen of Harry Dolman still proved astute. Always watching carefully the activities of the new board he sounded a note of caution as they spent money on top players to ensure Bristol City could compete at the top level.

He told friends and anyone who would listen: "If they carry on spending like that the club will be bankrupt within eight years."

Sadly his prediction was overly-optimistic. The club hit financial trouble in 1982, sending it into free-fall from the top flight down to the basement. During those dark days cash income from the bowling club in the Dolman Stand proved vital to keeping the club alive as it was used to pay off some of the most pressing debts, while a solution to the crisis was sought.

But the club was still flying high in August 1977 when Harry Dolman OBE celebrated his 80th birthday. A special tribute luncheon was held at the Holiday Inn, Bristol. Despite not being in the best of health Harry loved the attention and toasts in his honour and was proud that money was also being raised for the Under Privileged Children's Charity of the Variety Club of Great Britain.

Speeches were made recognising his contributions to both sport and industry in Bristol. It was one of the last occasions that Harry Dolman appeared in public as he passed away just three months later on November 9, 1977.

Around 1,000 people attended a memorial service in his honour at Bristol Cathedral a few weeks later and tributes poured in from the worlds of commerce and football.

In the Queen's Birthday Honours List in 2017 Marina was awarded an MBE for services to football. In the same honours the club's owner and major shareholder Steve Lansdown was awarded the CBE for his services to business and the community of Bristol.

Marina said: "It is a great surprise and I'm very, very honoured. Harry would laugh that I received an honour from the Queen for services to football while his OBE was for services to export business. It was only after we got together in 1961 that I started watching football after he insisted I go along with him.

"Now 56 years later football, and following Bristol City, is a major part of my life and I travel all over the country and have so many friends in football - all thanks to Harry."

In the last few months of his life Harry Dolman wrote on a small notebook his vision of football in the future. He predicted what it would be like in 2037 - 60 years after his death. Many of those thoughts have already come to fruition - some have not, but his vision makes fascinating reading and here are those predictions in full:

- All spectators will sit. There will be very little standing and some stands will be heated.
- Pitches will be artificial, no grass.
- Lighting will be better and as good as the best daylight.
- Four to six lights will light up each quarter of the pitch and will be positioned above the pitch.
- Turnstiles will be completely automatic.
- Pitches will be slightly raised, about six inches for perfect draining.
- No-one will stand or sit in the rain as all spectators will be under cover. In time pitches will be under cover as well.
- Clubs will become more professional at the top and will be much more heavily financed, paying dividends to shareholders.
- There will be less clubs in the English league but there will be more and more junior clubs under the jurisdiction of the Football League.
- Bristol City will be in a European league but a world league will be on the way and football will be spread out over the whole year.
- Referees will be more professional, full time and as well paid as most players.
- The laws of the game will change a little but not much. The greatest change will be in the penalty rules. The kick will be taken from the spot of the offence, but the penalty spot will still exist for certain offences.

- Football clubs will become big sports centres embracing bowls, squash, snooker, badminton, tennis and swimming under the large stands which will appear in grounds.

So many of the predictions have an echo in Bristol City's ground redevelopment in the 21st century, which saw the structure of the Dolman Stand retained and form the base of one side of the present day Ashton Gate, retaining Harry Dolman's name.

Although the bowls club moved out some years ago to its own purpose-built centre the concourse at the Dolman Stand has been used for boxing matches and has proved to be a major asset to the club as part of its hospitality and conference facilities. The ground now being home to Bristol Sport, incorporating Bristol Rugby, women's football and Bristol Flyers basketball team has proved Harry Dolman's vision of clubs becoming a centre for sport was correct.

The pitch, although not artificial, is a Deso pitch that includes plastic elements that enable it to be hard-wearing throughout a busy season. Turnstiles are indeed automatic and all top stadiums in the UK are now all-seater with superb floodlighting.

The man who could design a machine that would make millions; could sketch out a football stand on the back of a cigarette packet and see it through to fruition; and who had the ability to motivate others in business and sport was always looking forward to the future and how he might make a difference.

ACKNOWLEDGEMENTS

We would like to thank the following people who have provided information and services during the research of this book:

- Marina Dolman, Hazel Stone, Tony Dolman, Tom Hopegood, Andrew Billingham, Derek Andrews, Mike Lillington, Christine Lillington, William Powell, Philip Kirley, Johnny Watkins, Vivian Jenkins, Adam Baker, Steve Smith, David Woods, M Shed, Bristol Archives, Bristol City Football Club, Empica Public Relations

The following books proved useful in research and fact checking:

- The Bristol Babe, The First 100 Years of Bristol City FC: David M. Woods (Yore Publications)
- Bristol City, The Complete History of the Club: Peter Godsiff (Wensum Books)
- A Life of Two Halves, The Chris Garland Story: James Ryan & Mark Leesdad (Redcliffe)
- Bristol City, The Post War Years: David Woods (Desert Island Books)

The following websites were used for reference:
- British Newspaper Archive
- Hansard

PICTURE CREDITS

1st section

P1 Marina Dolman

P2 Top. Polunnio Ltd

P2 Middle. Graces Guide

P2 Bottom. Polunnio Ltd

P3 Top. Marina Dolman

P3 Left. Marina Dolman

P3 Right. Tony Dolman

P4 Marina Dolman

P5 Marina Dolman

P6/7 Tony Dolman

P8 Top. Bristol Archives 43207-19-4-002

P8 Middle. European Patent Office

P9 Bristol Archives 43207-2-050

P10 Derek Andrews

P11 Top. Bristol Archives 40826-PUB-006

P11 Left. www.junkyardcollectables.co.uk

P11 Right. Derek Andrews

P12 The Illustrated London News

P13 Top left. Tony Dolman

P13 Top right. John Penny

P13 Middle. Marina Dolman

P13 Bottom. Marina Dolman

P14 Marina Dolman

P15 Marina Dolman

P16 Marina Dolman

2nd section

P1 Top. David Woods

P1 Bottom. Marina Dolman

P2 Top. Marina Dolman

P2 Mike Lillington

P2 Bristol Archives 45556

P3 Marina Dolman

P4 Top left. Marina Dolman

P4 Top right. John Penny

P4 Bottom. Marina Dolman

P5 Top left. Derek Andrews

P5 Top right. Derek Andrews

P5 Bottom. Marina Dolman

P6 Marina Dolman

P7 Marina Dolman

P8 Marina Dolman

P9 Marina Dolman

P10 Marina Dolman

P11 Mike Lillington

P12 Top. Marina Dolman

P12 Bottom. Tony Dolman

P13 Martin Powell/Bristol Post

P14 Marina Dolman

P15 Steve Smith/Bristol Post

P16 Top. Marina Dolman

P16 Bottom. Bristol Archives GGBCFC 093 1977